The Time of the End

Daniel's Prophecy Reclaimed

Jay E. Adams

Milton C. Fisher

MID-AMERICA
INSTITUTE FOR NOUTHETIC STUDIES

Institute for Nouthetic Studies, a ministry of Mid-America Baptist Theological Seminary, 5640 Airline Road, Arlington, TN 38002
mabts.edu and nouthetic.org

ISBN: 978-1-970445-09-1 (Print)
ISBN: 978-1-970445-10-7 (eBook)
Old ISBN: 978-1-889032-21-2

Editor: Donn R. Arms

Library of Congress Cataloging-in-Publication Data
Names: Adams, Jay E., 1929 - 2020
Title: *The Time of the End: Daniel's Prophecy Reclaimed*
by Jay E. Adams and Milton C. Fisher
Description: Arlington, TN: Institute for Nouthetic Studies, 2025
Identifiers: ISBN 9781970445091 (paper)
Classification: LCC BS1555.5 .A18 | DDC 224.5

Published in the United States of America

Dedication

For all the saints who from their labors rest,
Who Thee, by faith, before the world confessed.
William Walsham How

Those who are wise shall shine
like the brightness of heaven's expanse,
And those who turn many to righteousness
like the stars forever and ever.
Daniel 12:3

And to each one of them was given a white robe
and they were told to rest for a little while longer
until the full number of their fellow slaves and
brothers who were about to be put to death,
as they also had been, was completed.
Revelation 6:11

CONTENTS

Foreword

In the Middle Ages it was a common sight to see a Latin edition of the Bible chained to the pulpit in a church. The chain was affixed to the book not to prevent robbery by thieves: it was there to protect the Bible from falling into the hands of unskilled laymen who might dare to read it and interpret it for themselves. During this epoch the Bible belonged to the clergy, who alone were equipped to plumb the depths of its content.

One of the revolutionary elements of the Protestant Reformation was the putting of the Bible into the hands of the people so that they could read it for themselves. The Bible was translated into the vernacular to facilitate this end. Martin Luther fought for the right of "private interpretation" of Scripture. Rome warned that the granting of such a privilege would "open a floodgate of iniquity" as people would inevitably distort the meaning of Scripture and interpret it in ways contrary to that of Holy Mother Church.

Luther countered this by insisting upon the doctrine of the perspicuity of Scripture, or its basic clarity, wherein the foundational teaching of the Gospel was plain enough for a child to understand, and its message was of such monumental importance as to warrant getting it into the hands of as many people as possible. This feat was made simple by a quantum leap in the means of production—the invention of a new tool called the printing press, that used the new technique of movable type. Luther clearly understood the dangers inherent in freeing the Bible from its chains, but weighed the advantages against the risks, concluding: "If a floodgate of iniquity be opened, so be it!"

Luther's view of private interpretation was not simplistic. He argued that with the *right* of private interpretation, comes also the *responsibility* of accurate interpretation. To guard against unbridled speculations and a relativistic approach to Scripture, the Reformers developed the so-called "Reformed hermeneutic." This rested upon the primary premise of the "analogy of faith" (*analogia fidei*), the principle that the Scripture is its own interpreter. In expounding his doctrine of the perspicuity of Scripture, Luther acknowledged that not all parts of Scripture are equally clear. The rule was to interpret the arcane in light of the clear, the implicit in light of the explicit. By subordinating the arcane to the clear, the plain sense of Scripture could triumph over bizarre and imaginative interpretations. The objectivity of the *grammatico-historical* interpretation would serve as a safeguard against subjectivism. Luther warned against fanatics who would turn the Bible into a waxed-nose, twisting and shaping it to suit their own bias. At this point Luther shared Rome's concern over the potential dangers of unleashing the floodgates of iniquity.

In a sense, Rome's alarm was prophetic. Subsequent history has indeed witnessed the twisting of Scripture into all sorts of wild and fanciful interpretations. This is nowhere more evident than in the realm of interpretation of Biblical prophecy. The "science" of eschatology has been bombarded with speculative theories that frequently transgress the borders of responsible interpretation.

Perhaps eschatology is the most vulnerable field of inquiry to Biblical distortion. This vulnerability is linked to several factors including the following:

1. Since eschatology involves future matters, it lacks the advantage of the 20–20 vision of hindsight. It is one thing to see fulfillment of ancient prophecies that were realized in the past, such as Old Testament prophecies that were fulfilled in New Testament times. It is quite another thing to see with equal clarity those prophecies that still await their fulfillment.
2. Biblical future prophecy is often set forth in a genre of literature called apocalyptic. This genre is often characterized by symbols and imaginative language, such as that found in the New Testament book of Revelation and the Old Testament book of Daniel. Because of the often arcane aspects of such symbolism, this mode of literature is often the most difficult to understand.
3. Future prophecy often lends itself to a kind of sensationalism that finds an eager audience and provokes avid followers. Since we are all concerned about our own future, we are quick to em-

brace a scenario that promises good news for us. Rosy promises tend to be popular.

One of the most popular eschatological theories in modern evangelicalism is that of the pre-tribulation rapture. This view has become the majority report in our day. It has been popularized by Hal Lindsey's runaway best-seller, *The Late Great Planet Earth,* and more recently by the multi-million sales of the novels coauthored by Tim LaHaye and Jerry Jenkins under the title *Left Behind.* Christian television daily trumpets this eschatology to the nation, yet I cannot name a single text in the Bible that provides a solid basis for affirming a pre-tribulation rapture. If ever there was an eschatological "house of cards," this is it.

It is against the backdrop of such bizarre speculations that have risen to such popularity that I find this exposition of Daniel so welcoming and refreshing. This book stresses the central motif of Daniel, the sovereignty of God over all of history. It is God who is seen as the central character of the book of Daniel. Daniel is the agent of divine revelation who, both in his life and in his prophetic visions, displays the reign of God by which He raises kings and kingdoms up and brings kings and kingdoms down.

In this volume, the book of Daniel is expounded with clarity, showing this Old Testament apocalypse to be in harmony with the New Testament book of Revelation.

The book explains carefully and soberly, following the principles set forth in Reformed hermeneutics, Daniel's visions concerning the great world emperors who were to come in God's plan of redemptive history. The five kingdoms are identified as

1. Babylon
2. Medo-Persia
3. Greece
4. Rome
5. the Messianic Kingdom of God.

Jay Adams and Milton Fisher do a sterling job in disclosing the meaning of the symbolism of Daniel. Their handling of the breakup of Alexander's empire among his four leading generals is most noteworthy. They correctly render the symbolism of the "little horn" in Daniel 8 as referring to Antiochus Epiphanes of Syria.

Perhaps the most interesting and gripping element of this book is its analysis of the highly controversial meaning of the "seventy weeks" of Daniel. The treatment of this question alone makes the reading of this book worthwhile and mandatory.

As the book of Daniel itself brings consolation to all who love the sovereignty of God, so this treatment of Daniel's book will serve as a strong reinforcement of that consolation. I am grateful for this careful and cogent labor of love.

R. C. Sproul
Orlando, 1999

Preface

Daniel! At the very sound of his name all sorts of associations well up: memories of Sunday School stories about the fiery furnace and the lions' den, encounters with Seventh Day Adventist prophetic charts, or something else. Whatever the notions that spring to mind, for nearly every Christian there has been more than one memorable contact with the prophecy of Daniel.

Yet, for all this familiarity with the book, to many who sing ever so lustily, "Dare to Be a Daniel," much of his prophecy is a closed book. It is hard to understand: full of mystery, strange visions, and dark sayings. If pressed to do so, they would find it difficult—perhaps impossible—even to begin to state the purpose for which the Holy Spirit inspired Daniel to write this unique book and for which He included it in the canon of sacred Scripture. They would be unable to summarize its contents or set forth its major themes. Beyond moralizing from some of its stories, they would be unable to use it properly as a guide for Christian living.

As you have read along so far, you may well have said to yourself, "I guess that pretty well describes me." If so, read on! Rest assured that we intend not only to open up the meaning of the book of Daniel for you, but also to help you see how its thrust and message can make a difference in your own life.

Commentaries on the book of Daniel abound, but sometimes their focus is narrowed to single trees and to the acorns on some branch, so as to avert your eyes from the forest. Then, too, excessive interest in the predictive element of the biblical prophecy has led others into a sensationalism that strives to link every vision and angelic dialogue found in Daniel to the latest newscast.

There has been, to be sure, a revival of concern with the prophetic writings of the Bible. This concern is healthy when it is not out of balance. Perhaps it is because some have gone overboard in their handling of prophetic material that there are now a great number of Christians who are looking for a sane approach to the interpretation of books like Daniel. Such persons deserve a clear, concise, and measured approach to the book.

Therefore, in *The Time of the End*, we have made every effort to overcome the problems we have mentioned. In doing so, we have not written another detailed commentary, but instead have addressed what we believe to be the major concerns and needs of anyone seeking to understand the intent and content of the book of Daniel. You will, of course, find a good bit of exposition and, in places where necessary to fulfill our aim, some more intense analysis of the text. But it is not our objective to fill your head with esoteric facts. It is rather to lay bare the overall message of Daniel, indicating its personal application to your life.

A word must be spoken in explanation of our subtitle, "Daniel's Prophecy Reclaimed." Through this entire century, and then some, many fascinating but fanciful interpretations and applications of Daniel's words have been proposed and propagated. Our book aims to restore a sane appreciation for the actual historical purpose and impact of this remarkable prophecy. Read on, and you'll see what we mean.

We send forth this book with the hope and prayer that God will use it to unlock a unique portion of His Word that ought to be open to far more readers than it has been. We want to challenge many in our day, similar in some ways to that in which Daniel lived and wrote, to see that "the Most High is sovereign Ruler over the kingdoms of men, and He gives them to whom He decrees." (Daniel 4:32b; Aramaic text, 4:29.)[1]

1 English translation of the Bible text throughout is that of the co-authors, rather than from randomly selected versions.

Introduction

So much could be said by way of introduction. But the basic issues concerning the date and authorship of the book and the validity of divinely inspired predictions such as it contains, crucial as they are in the struggle with unbelief and liberalism, have already occasioned rivers of printer's ink. Those discussions—and others related and worthwhile—would simply take us too far afield of our stated purpose, so we have reluctantly abandoned them. And although it would be fascinating to trace these battles, together with their resolutions, suffice it to state here that we are confident that the sixth-century Daniel wrote his own book—enabled by divine revelations to predict with amazing precision future events that even he could not comprehend at the time.

The concern here and throughout this study is to help you understand what the book of Daniel is all about. Once you have done that, you'll be able to utilize its truths in your everyday affairs. So our focus is on questions like, Why was the book written? How does the Holy Spirit intend to change us by it? And, very practically, how ought God's Word given through this prophet be preached, applied, and obeyed today?

Daniel is replete with fascinating stories, familiar to every wide-awake Sunday School student: the fiery furnace, the lions' den, the handwriting on the wall, and some other strange things. Yet as he reviews these stories, more often than not, the teacher majors on the minor themes. When the student hears about Daniel's faith or Nebuchadnezzar's pride, he learns (rightly, to be sure) that he ought not be proud, that he should trust God implicitly in every trial, and all the rest. But how often has the *major* note, to which all such overtones add depth and color, been sounded? It is almost like being taught to read the alto, bass, and tenor parts, which add harmony to the music, but not the melody!

Simply put, the book of Daniel was written as a handbook for persecuted believers. In it, the Holy Spirit provides comfort, encouragement, insight, and direction for those who will live during extremely difficult times ahead. He gives insight into the course of human history and the moving power behind all events. By demonstrating His care for His own during the Babylonian captivity, and how He expected them to act under persecution and trial, God provided guidance and hope for the future. Both Matthias (the Maccabean of the intertestamental period) and Jesus Himself, in the Olivet Discourse, used the book of Daniel to help believers in times of trial.

Daniel was written at a low point in the history of Israel, when she was in captivity and exile, to purify her of her sins. The prophecy was intended to show that, far from abandoning or forgetting His people, God was purging them. The unfolding history and fortunes of Babylon are shown to be simply God's means of dealing with His own, just as the prophets Isaiah, Jeremiah, and Ezekiel had anticipated. Moreover, God's control and direction of the present history was proof that in future times, when once again trials would intensify, God would still be at work. In foretelling the future, on a broad scale and in some cases in greater detail, Daniel assures us that not only the present, but also all of history—past and future—is under His sovereign control. Indeed, the key to the book is the oft-repeated theme (slightly varied from place to place) that "the Most High is sovereign Ruler over the kingdoms of men, and to whom He decrees He gives them" (Daniel 4:32b; compare also 2:37-38; 4:17, 25; 5:18, 21; 7:26-27).

There are two elements in this glorious affirmation that we should pause to consider. First, notice the title given to God: "The Most High." God was proclaiming to His own people and to the leaders of world empires that He, not they or their gods, was (and is)[1] *supreme*. He is first; no god, no thing, no human person is to be exalted to His place. Throughout the book, men, by their fabricated deities, attempted to prove otherwise by usurping divine prerogatives; but

1 In view of Scripture's teaching of the immutability of God, any observation about His state of being in the past is equally true in the present and future. This is assumed throughout, but statements about past events will use the past tense.

in the end, God forced them to admit that He alone was the true God of all creation.

God's people were at that time subject to Babylon, not because of *her* greatness, but because of His. It was God who had brought Babylon into greatness in order to bring about His own purposes through her. God had, with careful intent, placed His people into her rough hands. Human affairs—extending even to the rise and fall of empires—are ordered by Him for His purposes. Contrary to the then-current thought, the defeat of Israel did not mean the defeat of Israel's God. Nebuchadnezzar's downfall as a result of pride, for example, is not merely a lesson on the evils and consequences of personal pride. Rather, it is also the demonstration of the key theme of the book: God is supreme—even in Babylon the Great! The same theme is echoed in the story of Belshazzar, who gave praise to other gods (5:4) and was forced to admit (to his horror) that this supreme God held his life and all his ways in His hand (5:23). The point of the story is made quite clear in 5:18-28. No one else can take His place.

This is an important truth for God's people to learn—then and now. It was because of their idolatry and its attendant evils that God brought His people into exile (2 Chronicles 36:14-21). He was at work rooting out every vestige of this prime sin from among them. By forcing their captors to admit the failure of their idols and to confess that Jehovah was supreme, He vividly showed His own people the futility of paganism. At the same time, of course, He made the truth apparent to the idolaters themselves. This dual focus is highlighted by a distinctive literary feature of the book of Daniel. It was written in two languages, Hebrew and Aramaic—one portion directed primarily to God's people, the other to the nations.

The second thing we must note is that God declares His sovereignty. One must acknowledge Him not only as supreme, but also as Sovereign. Here, too, the twofold viewpoint of the book is significant. It strongly affirms that history is not out of control. At times, one might be tempted to think so, as the original readers might have, considering their affliction and subjugation. But Daniel teaches us that what happens is according to God's design. *He* brought down their power and destroyed their kingdom through Nebuchadnezzar, His servant. On the other hand, to Nebuchadnezzar and to the rulers of the empires that followed his, the revelation of God's sovereignty communicated, "You are not the self-made power you think you are. Rather, you are an agent of the supreme God, raised up to bring honor to His name and blessing to His people—whether you on your own realize and acknowledge this or not. By faith or by force, you will do so—to His glory!"

Both of those messages are sorely needed today. We will not develop this dual theme at this point, but perhaps it ought to be said, however, that the days might not be too distant when God's people in the English-speaking world will once again discover the importance of acknowledging both God's supremacy and sovereignty, in an era when all outward circumstances may seem to indicate otherwise. World history, ever since Daniel's time, has shown that those rulers who failed to do so soon encountered the consequences of their failure.

The same is true of the church. The confusion and turmoil among leaders in churches today, as well as among the world's political leaders, is the fruit of idolatrous humanism, which seeks to find supremacy and sovereignty in man. Evolutionary thinking and the practically universal adoption of the self-love, self-esteem teachings of the world clearly demonstrate the church's humanistic bent today, a bent that is idolatrous.

So the main point to keep in the forefront of your mind as you study about Daniel's book is that it contains two messages, based upon one dual theme: God's supremacy and sovereignty. One is directed to world leaders—"Acknowledge Him thus, or else!" The other is to His people—"Repent and take heart; God is ordering history for your purification, as well as for His honor and glory."

Beyond and above all that has been said so far stands a more specific, a more essential and crucial element, an aim that gives meaning and focus to the whole. The supremacy and sovereignty of God, the book shows, is most clearly and gloriously demonstrated in the coming of the Messiah, God's Son, whose everlasting empire supersedes the world empires existing prior to it. Each one—Babylon, Medo-Persia, Greece, and even "eternal" Rome—was forced to realize that it could not (in Satan's name and might) establish a truly worldwide empire composed of people from every tribe and tongue and nation. None of these emperors was ever supreme, the sovereign over all, because Satan couldn't be either.

Nor were those historic empires, for all their apparent power and grandeur, able to last. One gave way to the next, in turn, and ultimately the whole earthly structure came tumbling down under blows from a stone cut out, though not by (human) hands (Daniel 2:34, 45). Ultimately, each was brought to the realization of the truth. None could take the place and the prerogatives of God. One way or another, each found it necessary to confess grudgingly that the God of Israel, the God of the Bible, was the one and only supreme Sovereign. As was apparent long before, when God scattered the nations through the confusion of tongues, all of Satan's efforts to counter that reality would be in vain. Only the King of kings and Lord of lords could bring together an empire like "a mountainous boulder that fills all the earth" (Daniel 2:35).

Only a truly worldwide, continuing empire, with a truly divine head, could rightly fulfill the requirements for absolute supremacy and sovereignty. And it was that toward which all of this confrontation with the Satanic empires was leading. God placed Daniel where he could speak to friend and foe alike about these things. At the culmination of Satan's sway over the Gentile nations, *at the time of the end*, after Satan had had plenty of time to do his worst, the God of Heaven set up the true empire through the advent of Jesus Christ. It alone is the eternal empire that will not pass to another, and it grows from a small beginning to extend into all the earth. It is the first and only truly world empire in all of history. (Note again, Daniel 2:35c, 44-45.) There has never been anything like it, an empire composed of a new and redeemed people.

So, at last, we arrive at the grandest theme of all—the one that integrates the rest. According to a predetermined schedule (cf. Daniel 2:44 and 9:25), God set His Son as the God-man upon the throne of this worldwide kingdom (Daniel 7:13-14), thus demonstrating for all time and eternity Who is truly supreme and sovereign. And, from that time on, His people reign with Him (7:18).

This, then, is what the book of Daniel is all about. It's about Jesus Christ, King of kings and Lord of lords, Emperor of the World.

General Analysis and Overview

A century before Daniel's birth, the Assyrians had carried off a large portion of the Northern Kingdom of Israel, a judgment for their apostasy and sin. Throughout the years following, the Southern Kingdom of Judah became more and more like her sister Israel. Her iniquity increased until God declared her beyond all remedy (2 Chronicles 36:16b; read vv. 14-21 for the full account, and cf. Jeremiah 25:3-11). So God judged Judah too.

In three invasions, 605 BC (when Daniel was carried off to Babylon), 597 BC (when another 10,000 captives were deported), and 587/6 BC (when the city of Jerusalem and the temple of Solomon were destroyed), the Babylonians swept down upon her, smashing her as with successive blows of a hammer (Jeremiah 50:23). This was no freak event of history. God in His providence, as we've already seen, raised up Babylon as a force to discipline His people and purge them of idolatry. When it was all over there was hardly a trace left of the former Hebrew kingdom.

The book of Daniel, written while the people were still exiles in Babylon, was intended to encourage them to repent and prepare for the future, when God would return them to their land. We must again take note of its peculiar literary form. A lengthy section at the center of the book (2:4b-ch. 7) was composed in Aramaic, at that time the language of world diplomacy. Therein is declared God's supreme sovereignty over all nations. But the rest of the chapters, dealing with matters relating directly to the Jewish people and how world affairs would involve and affect them up to the time of Messiah, are written in Hebrew. This is the part intended to strengthen and guide God's people through the difficult times to come. The message not only provided comfort and encouragement by declaring that future trials were not outside God's control, but it also unmistakably showed that God was the God of history, for He could "pre-write" it.

Each major section has its own "key" chapter, setting forth the course of world empires. They are:

1. Chapter Two: disclosing the course of pagan world dominion up until the time of Christ, Whose empire will destroy and replace them all.
2. Chapter Nine: predicting the restoration of God's people to their land, with a timetable of the period reaching to the coming of Jesus Christ.

In addition to the fact that the book of Daniel is written in both Hebrew and Aramaic, it is also unusual in that much of its message is presented in apocalyptic form. There are only two true apocalypses in the Bible—Daniel and Revelation. A few of the other books contain brief apocalyptic sections. But these two books stand in especially close relationship to each other.

The apocalyptic genre (well known outside of the Bible in Jewish writings) teaches through symbols and visions, more or less self-interpreted for the reader who carefully looks for clues. The symbols employed in apocalyptic scenes represent specific persons, nations, and events. Those who seek to understand the material, therefore, must approach apocalyptic literature according to its own principles of interpretation. They cannot deal with it as they would with simple narrative, poetry, or epistolary literature—each of which has its special rules of interpretation. In Daniel, as you recall, the prophetic portions are mostly symbolic. The giant image, the rock, and the strange animals and their horns immediately come to mind.

After chapter one's introductory narrative in Hebrew, the book follows a two-part division by language.

Analytical Outline

Chapter One: Introduction (Hebrew)

Part One (Aramaic)

A. Ch. 2 The Dream
B. Ch. 3 The Fiery Furnace
C. Ch. 4 Nebuchadnezzar's Edict
D. Ch. 5 The Handwriting on the Wall
E. Ch. 6 The Lions' Den
F. Ch. 7 The Judgment of World Empires and Founding of God's Empire through Christ

Part Two (Hebrew)

A. Ch. 8 Medo-Persia and Greece;
The Great Enemy of God's People and the Destruction of the Sanctuary
B. Ch. 9 Daniel's Prayer; 70 Heptad Timetable
C Ch. 10-12 Contacts and Conflicts between God's People and the Greek Empire:
    1. Daniel's concern here is with the 3rd of the world empires, Greece. (He was living mainly in the time of Babylon, the first of the four.)
    2. God's people would suffer great trials at the hands of the third.
    3. They would need strength then,
        a. by seeing how God carried His people safely through previous periods of world upheaval;
        b. by seeing that nothing was out of God's control, but was, on the contrary, happening precisely as He predicted it would.
    4. No need for him to discuss the 4th world empire in great detail, since
        a. the events were much farther off, and
        b. the book of Revelation would expand truth about the 4th and 5th empires.

Some of the repetition in Daniel's book (besides adding new facts) stems from the fact that the revelation was not all given at the same time. Daniel received God's messages over a seventy-year period, often with great gaps of time between visions. People receiving additional parts of Daniel's message would need some background information in order to grasp its intent.

The following diagram displays some of the major points of the book:

COMMENTS:

Observe *two* sets of prophecies:

Chapters 2 through 7 = course of world empire, in relation to God's Kingdom—given in the Aramaic language.

Chapters 8 and 11-12 = limited period of the next-to-come (3rd, Greek) empire; persecution of Jews by neighbors—in Hebrew.

Distinguish the two "little horn" persecutions accordingly.

Image (Basic)	**Beasts** (Distinctives)			
Chapters 1,2	Chapter 7	Chapter 8	Chapter 9	Chaps 10-12
Part 1--Aramaic 2:4b-7:28		Part 2--Hebrew 8:1-12:13		
Gold Babylon	**Lion** winged			
Silver Medo-Persia	**Bear** raised on one side: Persia over Media (3 ribs: Egypt, Lydia, & Babylon	**Ram** 22 horns, one higher: Persia over Media		
Brass Greece	**Leopard** with 4 heads; 4 parts of Alexander's kingdom-split	**He-Goat** from West Notable horn =Alexander; 4 horns = 4 generals; 1 little horn= Antiochus Ephiphanes of Syria		**Kings** of third Empire: N.= Syria:: the Seleucids; S.=Egypt: Ptolemies (11:21, Antio-chus of Syria
Iron/Tile Rome	**Monster** with 10 horns & 1 little horn: Roman Empire		**Rome** and	
Stone Kingdom of God **Negative** Destruction	**Kingdom** taken from beasts; given to Christ and His people at the ascension: vv. 10-12, 21-22, 26-27 **Positive** Setting Up		the **Messiah** (Earthly Jerusalem destroyed)	

Chapter 1
God and the King's Diet

In our Overview we mentioned that God's people suffered deportation from Judah in three separate waves, subsequent to that of the Northern Kingdom of Israel in 722 BC. In 605 BC, Daniel was one of those carried off as part of the first group. He was one of the relatively few taken at this first attack on Jerusalem by the Babylonian emperor, Nebuchadnezzar. The number apparently was limited to "Israelites of the royal seed and nobility," the very best the declining nation had to offer, so that they might learn and serve the palace (Daniel 1:3-4). In addition to the service they might render the court, these young boys (Daniel may have been about fourteen years of age) were likely being held as hostages.

Yet the chapter opens, not with the carrying off of Daniel and his friends, but with the removal of the vessels from the temple of God in Jerusalem (v. 2). Emphasis upon this event is not incidental. It not only sets the scene for the dramatic event of chapter five, but it also essentially raises the critical issue of this book.

When a conquering king would loot a neighboring peoples' temple of precious items after having subdued them, he meant to show that his god was greater than those whose temples he plundered. Israel's faith, of course, was monotheistic. Jehovah her God was alone God of the universe. Henotheism is the doctrine that each nation has its own god. That's how Nebuchadnezzar viewed Israel: that Jehovah was merely Israel's god. And while Babylon was polytheistic (some thirteen principal deities in their pantheon), they assumed that foreign gods had power only in the country where they were worshipped. The book of Daniel demonstrates the falsehood of such ideas.

However, the point of the chapter, as well as that of the entire book, is that Jehovah, the only true God, has *not* been defeated. He is superior to the gods of all the nations, and in fact raises up and uses nations for His own purposes.

The king of Babylon, the ruler of an empire, thought he was in control of history, making the history of his day according to his own plans. But God was in control, using Nebuchadnezzar as His whip to discipline and purify His people (cf. Jeremiah 25:3-11; 2 Chronicles 36:15-21). Again and again throughout the book of Daniel, the sovereignty of God over the nations and over the affairs of men is made clear. Starting with this chapter, this truth appears prominently:

> *The Lord delivered Jehoiakim … and a portion of the vessels belonging to the house of God….* (v. 2)
> *Now God caused Daniel to gain the good will and sympathy of the chief official….* (v. 9)
> *And to all four of these young men God gave knowledge and skill in all manner of learning and wisdom….* (v. 17)

As we continue on through the book, we shall observe this emphasis—the key message of the book—as it reappears, time and again. Above all else *God alone is sovereign,* and He forces the kings of the earth to acknowledge this truth. That is the distinctive note sounded throughout the book of Daniel.

Therefore, these details at the very beginning of the book are highly significant. As the extraordinary episodes of the book unfold, Jehovah is vividly portrayed, over against the gods of the nations, as the "God of Heaven" and "the Most High God," Creator and Sustainer of all peoples and all things. And the rulers of the nations are eventually brought to acknowledge that fact. Jehovah is not the god of Palestine alone, as those pagan rulers thought; He is the God Who has absolute control of the universe.

When Nebuchadnezzar took the temple articles, he did not understand God's sovereignty; he was thinking henotheistically. So, thinking he would honor the god of Babylon, he dedicated them to "his god" by putting them "into the treasure house of his god" (v. 2).

As we noted, this is not the last we shall hear of these temple treasures. Later, when God wanted to make a point of His sovereignty to Belshazzar by punishing him for his drunken rebellion (even though he should have known better), He did so in connection with these sacred vessels (cf. 5:1-4, 22-23). It becomes altogether clear who is in control. On that occasion, divine sovereignty is expressed in this way:

> *But you have not honored the God in Whose hand is your breath and to Whom belong all your ways.* (5:23b)

Here we make only a brief reference; in chapter five we shall say more. But do note how Daniel is already painting pertinent details into the picture, details which indeed play an important part later in his book. That is his method.

Does it surprise you that God is involved in politics? It is He Who brings down one ruler and sets up another. Perhaps to us His hand is not always so apparent and His purposes so clear as in this book. But that is one reason the book was written—to interpret history and politics for us. God intends to show us that all of history is a part of His great plan, designed to bring glory to His Name and to further His purposes. If it has anything to say, the book of Daniel tells us that God is the moving force behind world history. Hegel set forth his triadic view of history, Marx his thesis. While from a purely human perspective, such factors may bear some weight, they do so only because God uses them as elements in achieving His purposes. The God of heaven is at work bringing about His wishes and making His nature known.[11]

Consider, now, the main episode appearing in this chapter, "God and the King's Diet." Notice, we have not said, "*Daniel* and the King's Diet." Why not? Although Daniel was truly a faithful and courageous servant of Jehovah, who deserves all the praise ever heaped upon him and whose life should be emulated by every Christian, nevertheless, this episode, and the rest of the fascinating ones in the book, are not primarily about Daniel. They all have to do with Jehovah and the so-called gods of the heathen world. To see it otherwise is to make the book merely a record of moralistic tales.

This episode concerning the diet offered to Daniel and his companions can best be viewed from the perspective of three *purposes*:

1 [1] For more insight into the manifestation of God's nature as the dynamic behind world history, see *The Grand Demonstration*, by Jay E. Adams.

1. The King's purpose (vv. 3-7)
2. Daniel's purpose (vv. 8-16)
3. God's purpose (vv. 17-21)

All three purposes are, of course, interrelated, since God was at work in and through them. But the *emphasis* in the chapter is on what God did to cause the unusual result which we see take place in the life and health of Daniel and his companions.

This emphasis on the preeminence of God does not detract from the honor given Daniel in Scripture. Amazingly, not a single thing wrong is recorded about Daniel, while the sins of Abraham, Moses, and David are freely described. Daniel was truly exemplary.

The King's Purpose

The king's plan is spelled out in verses 3 to 5. He ordered Ashpenaz, chief of his court officials, to select from among the deportees of the royal line of Israel some young men (not "children," as the KJV says) who were physically well-endowed, intellectually sharp, well educated, and altogether qualified to serve in his court.

The king told Ashpenaz to teach them the language and lore of Babylon, presumably to "Babylonize" them—fit them for future service. Giving them Babylonian (Akkadian) names was another step in the same direction. And to see that they received the best of care, he assigned them the same food that he himself ate. Finally, after some three years of what we would call a liberal arts education, they would be ready to enter the king's service ("stand before the king," v. 5).

From the king's perspective it was a good plan. He would benefit not only from the wisdom and abilities of his Babylonian servants (including the Chaldean or Aramaean immigrants), but also from Israel's finest. He was attempting, as we said, to thoroughly Babylonize them, to totally change their ideas and customs.

Daniel's Purpose

But Daniel also had a purpose. We read, "But Daniel resolved, purposed (lit., set upon his heart = strong determination) not to defile himself ..." (v. 8). This young man, Daniel, was above all a conscientious servant of the living God. His purpose, therefore, differed from the king's. He intended to remain faithful to Jehovah. Above all, this would mean not compromising biblical restrictions as he served the king *under* Jehovah. Daniel's thinking was God first, the king second. He is presented all through the book of Daniel as *the man who would not compromise.* The book will show that neither fear nor favor was a strong enough motivation for Daniel to ever turn his back on the God Whom he worshipped.

There are a number of secondary elements involved in Daniel's confrontation with Ashpenaz that might be mentioned. We shall discuss a few.

To begin with, Hebrew dietary laws forbade certain foods that were served at the Babylonian king's table. Daniel was fully aware of this and determined not to "defile" himself by eating them (v. 8). Obviously he could not eat pork, shellfish, etc. But why could he not drink the king's wine? It was not because of abstinence, as some would have it. Faithful Hebrews did drink wine mixed with water. But the Babylonian custom was to offer the first part of their drink as a libation to their gods. For Daniel to drink with the rest, therefore, would mean he was participating in an idolatrous act. He therefore resolved to drink only water and to follow entirely another diet.

Take note of the interesting progression of thought in verses 8 and 9. "Daniel resolved … so he sought [permission] from the chief official…. Now God caused Daniel to gain the good will…." There was no need for Daniel to stage a showdown. He simply presented a reasonable alternative in the form of a test (vv. 11–14). Later on, of course, we see Daniel and his friends standing firm against direct orders that they could not obey without compromising their beliefs. So there are times to have a showdown as well as times not to. How can you know which is called for? We'll fully discuss this important distinction when we come to the incidents involving the fiery furnace and the lions' den. But for now, at least, we can see clearly that we do not necessarily have to alienate ourselves from unbelievers and bring down their wrath upon us if there is a righteous, honorable, and uncompromising alternative. We are not to go around needlessly creating issues and causing friction, as some do. As for how to present a possible alternative, observe the humility, courtesy, and respect demonstrated by Daniel (vv. 8, 12).

This has a bearing on activist Christian protestors, does it not, as to the rightness of their forcing confrontations and initiating legal action in the effort to pressure a pagan government to do things their way? Some modern tactics, and even some of the goals, may at times be less founded on clear biblical precepts and examples than even those of Gandhi and other modern movements. You must heed the caution of our Lord: "I am sending you out like sheep in the midst of wolves. So be wise as snakes and as harmless as doves" (Matthew 10:16). Romans 12:18 spells out the application of this divine imperative. The believer is at all times to do all *he* can to "be at peace with everybody." We shall see later under what circumstances it is not possible to do so.

After ten days the results came in. Daniel and his companions "looked healthier and better nourished" (v. 15) than those who had eaten the royal diet. Is this said to recommend for us all a strictly vegetarian diet, as some have concluded? Certainly not. Consistent with the total thrust of the book, it was God, not the diet, that made the difference. Throughout the chapter and the entire book, God is the chief Actor as we have seen (cf., for instance, vv. 9 and 17). The results of this test were as much the supernatural work of God as were the events at the fiery furnace and in the lions' den. All of this brings us to the central fact that God had a purpose.

God's Purpose

God's purpose was neither to teach the supposed virtues of vegetarianism nor to extol Daniel as a courageous and faithful youth. Daniel's thoughts were guided and his actions were motivated by the Holy Spirit, and are therefore exemplary, but God's purpose in all this was larger. What was it?

During those three years of training, God was also preparing Daniel for his life's work. He would become not only a wise advisor to kings, but also, principally, a minister of God in kings' courts. His task would be to make God known to pagan rulers and nations. These rulers would be brought into such close touch with God and His people that they would be caused to respond in ways that would further God's purposes in world history and, in particular, in the history of His people. Daniel and his companions would be called upon to vindicate God's sovereignty by their own lives and lips before world emperors and empires.

In addition, Daniel would bring messages of comfort, encouragement, and direction to the captive Hebrews. By interpreting God-given dreams that pointed to the future course of history, he would show rulers and God's people alike that Jehovah is the God of creation and providence. Hence, as the countdown progressed and the timetable he had sketched out (sometimes in the greatest detail) actually came to pass, the people of God could take heart. They could know that nothing had gone amiss, even as they encountered hardship and persecution. All through those momentous years, up to the coming of Christ and the establishment of *His* kingdom, Daniel's prophecies served as a guide to the unfolding of world history, its course, and its meaning. Nothing so sustained them through their trials as this.

God demonstrated that for His own purposes He could set His own in high places without compromise. Today, when politics universally has become so "dirty" and so much a matter of graft and compromise, it is hard to imagine anyone as pure and unsullied as Daniel rising to a place of influence. But here's the evidence that it is possible. Then, of course, it is only proper to notice that of all the deportees ("from among them" v. 6), there were only four who didn't compromise. Today, we can hardly expect larger numbers, can we? Nevertheless, the God of history can move the hearts even of unbelieving officials to turn things His way (v. 9).

Chapters 2 and 7
The Image, the Beasts, and the Stone

The second and seventh chapters of the book of Daniel are fundamental to any interpretation of the predictive prophecies of the book. Since they both sketch the broad outlines and form the essential framework for the more detailed prophecies that follow, and because jointly they concern matters clearly parallel to one another (yet in a way that they amplify and clarify one another), it will be useful to consider them together.

In fantastic apocalyptic dream-symbols and visions, the book of Daniel displays the general course of world history, from the days of Babylon up to the coming of the empire of God. These symbols stand for specific persons, nations, forces, and events. Obviously, as Daniel's interpretation of the dream in chapter two shows, the symbols themselves are not to be taken literally. Interpreting all, or even most, prophecy which was given in apocalyptic form in a literal (physical) manner leads to absurdity.

First we will study Nebuchadnezzar's dream, described in chapter two. The huge image in the dream was made up of four metallic elements, and the fifth element was a big stone. The following illustration will help you visualize the nature and composition of the image and the dramatic sequel to the dream. With Nebuchadnezzar's dream in mind, interpretation is easy.

God enabled Daniel to interpret the dream-vision. The reader is not left to his own ingenuity. Each of the five elements in the dream stands for a world empire. The first four represent successive worldly (Satanic) empires. They are, at the same time, both separate entities and parts of a whole. Together they constitute *one* image. This unity, clearly emphasized here in chapter two, declares that one power is at work behind them.

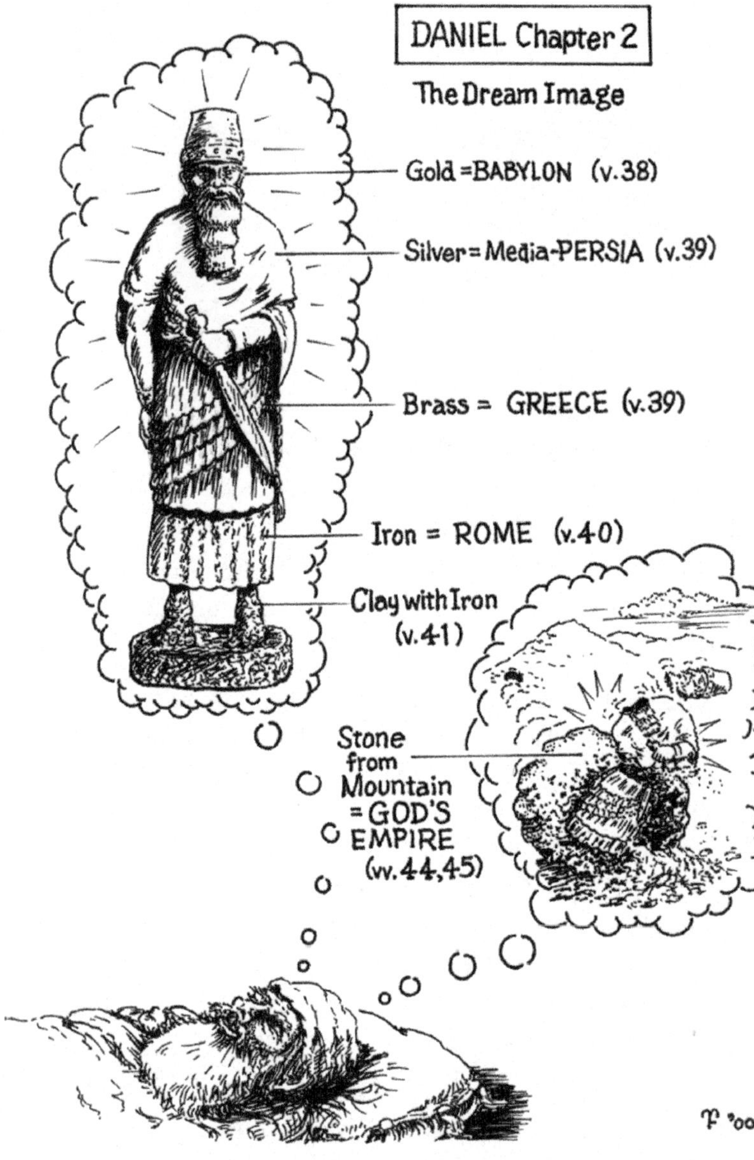

The fifth element stands alone, apart from and opposed to the image. It is disjunctive. Unlike the previous four empires, it is not just one more of the same kind. Yet in one sense, it is like the other elements—it too represents an empire.

How, then, does the fifth element differ from the other four? It is an empire of a very different nature. The first four are human, part of an autonomous but unsuccessful attempt by Satan to organize all society into one all-inclusive world empire under his rule. True, each covered a widening area of the earth. Yet the successive stages, represented by the four parts of the image, show a progressive weakening of quality and of inner strength—gold to silver to bronze to iron mixed with clay. The stone, however, was nonmetallic and natural in form. It was cut directly from the mountain, but not with human hands. Its form and function were divinely ordained and employed.

What, exactly, do the four-part image and the stone represent? The head of gold, as revealed by God, is the empire of Nebuchadnezzar the dreamer. It is Babylon. The rest, more fully explained in chapters seven and eight, are as follows. The chest and arms of silver = the empire of Medo-Persia, the thighs of bronze = the empire of Greece, and the clay and iron legs and feet = Rome. The supernaturally hewn stone is the empire of God (2:44-45). Unlike the previous four empires, it is a lasting one—it "will never be destroyed, and it will not be abandoned to another people."

To capture an overview, consider the following excerpt.

> When God created man, He placed the world under his (subordinate) authority. It was a derived dominion. God never has surrendered His ultimate sovereignty over creation and providence. Man's authority was a gracious gift of God, subservient to God's. This is plainly stated in Genesis 1:26-28:
>
> "And God said, Let us make man in our image, after our likeness: and let them have dominion … over all the earth … And God blessed them, and God said unto them, Be fruitful, and multiply, and replenish the earth, and subdue it: and have dominion … over every living thing that moveth upon the earth."
>
> But then man sinned. By this rebellion, in effect, man turned over to Satan the God-given dominion with which he was entrusted. Man abdicated the throne of world dominion, in favor of the rule of the evil one. Calvin wrote,
>
> The four beasts (of Daniel 7) took upon themselves the empire which properly belonged to the sacred lofty ones; that is, to God's elect sons.[1]

1 John Calvin, *Commentary on Daniel* (Grand Rapids: Eerdmans, 1948), II, p. 52.

Instead of reigning as king of the world, man became a slave to it. Instead of subduing the earth, he chose to be subdued by it. In all this he placed himself, and thereby his kingly authority, in the power of the devil. The latter lost no time ascending the throne.

Asserting his new authority, Satan in time founded, built up, and ruled over the first world empire in history: Babylon. Iniquity and the name of this world-dominating kingdom have become proverbially synonymous. Through this world-conquering kingdom Satan attempted to spread darkness like a thick smog across the face of the entire human race. In this he all but succeeded. But not quite. The God of heaven lit a lamp in the vast darkness. At first, God worked with a godly line of chosen individuals, whom He saved, and through whom He began revealing Himself and His purposes.

From the beginning He made known His great purpose to send a Savior. Even in that early patriarchal period He predicted larger horizons for the future: "in thee shall all the nations of the earth be blessed." Choosing the nation of Israel in grace (not because it was in itself any better than the rest of the nations), He established Israel as an outpost in the midst of what had become enemy territory. From this vantage point He planned to send forth a steady stream of "propaganda," by means of precept and example, and, in the fullness of time, to raise up One who would launch an attack that would defeat sin and Satan, redeem His own from eternal punishment, and restore man's rightful authority which was lost in the fall. The God of heaven continued to bring His program to pass. To Abraham, and later to Daniel, He revealed His purpose to establish a worldwide kingdom to replace the Satanic empire.

Daniel, in summary fashion, records and predicts the story of Babylon and Satan's three more successive world-kingdoms (see especially Daniel 2 and 7). By the metallic image, he shows how these kingdoms, in an attempt to expand with the ever-enlarging population of the earth, became each one inferior to the previous. From golden Babylon till iron-and-tile Rome, God was waiting.

Then, "in the days of those kings" (Dan. 2:44), He invaded the enemy's territory, conquered him and his forces (cf. Dan. 7:12), and bound him so that he could no longer deceive the Gentiles (or nations, as a whole) as he had in Old Testament times, until the "thousand years" (or N. T. age) were completed. In place of the demolished world-kingdom, He set up the kingdom of God, which is the eternal spiritual kingdom, visibly represented during the thousand years by the church.

Today this kingdom, which began as a small and insignificant entity like a mustard seed, is growing into a large, full-sized tree. Or, to use Daniel's figure, like an expanding stone, it is in the process of filling the whole earth. This is not to be understood in the postmillennial sense, that the whole world will be converted. But it does mean that the church is reaching into all corners of the world as the gospel is preached to every tribe, tongue, and nation. It means the kingdom Daniel predicted would become worldwide is actually becoming just that.

It was this kingdom that John and Jesus both announced as "at hand." It was not still hundreds of years off in the future. This is the kingdom to which Jesus gave Peter the keys, which the latter used to unlock its door for the Jews on the Day of Pentecost and for the Gentiles in the house of Cornelius. This is the kingdom of which Jesus spoke to Nicodemus in private, and to the multitudes in public. It is the kingdom *in* the world, but which He said was "not *of* this world." It is the worldwide mediatorial kingdom that He received at His ascension (Acts 2:36; Heb. 2:9; cf. Daniel 7:14), and of which He spoke after His resurrection (Acts 1:3).

The expansion of this kingdom was His concern when He gave the Great Commission, in Matthew 28:18-20:

"All authority hath been given unto me in heaven and on earth. Go ye therefore, and make disciples of all nations, baptizing them in the name of the Father and of the Son and of the Holy Spirit: teaching them to observe all things whatsoever I commanded you...."

Therein Jesus asserted the newly-granted authority that had been given to Him as the Messiah, because of His sacrifice on Calvary. As the Christ, of course, He had from all eternity been in possession of "all power." However, in His representative role as our Head, "he went up into heaven to receive gifts for men," and "as God-man he is advanced to the highest favor with God the Father." (*The Larger Catechism*, of the *The Westminster Confession*, Answers 53 and 54.)

On the basis of this unlimited authority over the nations (the "therefore" in verse 19 is significant), He sent forth His disciples into *all nations*—into territory which before had been "deceived" by Satan, under whose usurped authority they had previously served. In accordance with this, they went out preaching the gospel of the kingdom, praying, "Thy kingdom come." As a result of this tremendous onslaught, Rome, the last Satanic world-kingdom that history has known, fell, and "the kingdom of the world [became] the kingdom of our Lord, and of his Christ" (Rev. 11:15). Is it any wonder, then, that the elders sing,

> *"thou wast slain, and didst purchase unto God with thy blood men of every tribe, and tongue, and people, and nation, and madest them to be unto our God a kingdom and priests; and they shall reign upon the earth" (Rev. 5:9-10)?*[2]

Now, let's examine the symbolism of chapter two a bit more closely. Gold is an appropriate metal by which to represent Babylon. Nebuchadnezzar's lavish building program included much gold. Every school child knows about the famous hanging gardens of Babylon, but the city had many other remarkable features as well. Nebuchadnezzar himself once said (the inscription has been recovered) that nothing was too precious to be bestowed upon his great Babylon. Aeschylus, a 5th-century BC Greek dramatist, spoke of Babylon as "teeming with gold." And the historian Herodotus tells us that on top of the ziggurat (gigantic tower built in tiers, like the layers of a huge wedding cake) was a small shrine with a solid gold table inside. Below was a temple, with a golden image of Babylon's patron god, Marduk, seated upon a throne of gold upon a golden base, with a gold table in front of that. And outside the temple was an altar of solid gold. When we look at chapter three, we'll be confronted with an enormous golden image (perhaps confirmed by Herodotus, where he reports that it, or a similar one, was removed by Xerxes). No wonder Jeremiah spoke of Babylon as "a golden cup in Jehovah's hand" (51:7) and Isaiah called her "the golden city" (14:4)!

2 From Jay E. Adams, *The Time Is At Hand.* This book deals with prophecy in general and the book of Revelation in particular. Some minor changes have been made in this citation from pp. 56-60.

Silver is likewise appropriate for Persia. The Persians themselves referred to their personal worth in terms of their silver money. Their kings seemed to be bent on but one aim—amassing as much silver as possible. This was achieved through conquest and systematic taxation. Consequently, Persia was renowned more for her wealth than for her magnificence. Coinage came to Persia just shortly before Darius I became emperor, and so it was from him that the famous Persian coin, "daric," got its name. This amassing of wealth and consequent power by the successive Persian kings is noted in Daniel 11:2 as the prelude to their downfall, confrontation with Greece, and eventual conquest by Alexander.

Brass, in turn, is a fitting symbol for Greece. The bronze armor of the Greek hoplites (foot soldiers) was famous throughout the Mediterranean world. Josephus calls Alexander "a king from the west, clad in bronze" (*Antiquities*, 10:10:4). In another place he refers to the Greek armies as "men of bronze, coming from the sea."

The iron and baked clay, for Rome, is a bit more elusive. At the time Daniel wrote (6th century BC), Rome was but an infant city-state. But the day was coming when the *distinctive weapon* of the vast Roman armies would be the dreaded iron-headed pilum (a type of pike or javelin). However, the strength illustrated by iron was mixed in a noncohesive manner with clay, indicating weak or disruptive internal elements. Rome's generals were strong, but the central government was often chaotic. Assassinations, disorder, and changes in leadership were common.

Last comes the empire of God. Most humble of them all at its inception, its strength is internal because it is by the supernatural work of God's Spirit. By contrast, it is represented not by a metal (refined, molded, and fashioned by human beings and highly valued by them), but by a stone. Yet this stony empire, with its unlikely beginning, strikes the feet of the grand image. The latter comes crashing to the ground. Smashed and pulverized to a fine powder, it is blown away like chaff. The stone grows till it becomes a huge mountain which, in time, fills the whole earth (2:34-35).

Babylonian writings refer to a "mountain stone" with a sense of awe. For them, dwellers on a flat plain, mountains were impressive. It is assumed that the Mesopotamians' ziggurats were built in imitation of their missing mountains. Nebuchadnezzar even speaks of his works as "mountain high." He did, in fact, build the hanging gardens for his wife, to remind her of the mountains in her native Media.

Chapter Seven

The dream that Daniel was given is recorded in chapter seven. Its revelation covers the same period of time as that of chapter two and relates to the same five empires. Take note that the Aramaic (*international*) section of the book (2:4-7:28) thus begins and concludes with a similar or parallel prophecy. The seventh chapter is likewise made up of two sections: (1) The Dream (vv. 1-14) and (2) Its Interpretation (vv. 15-28). And, significantly, it is the transitional chapter that both summarizes what comes before and points forward to further prophetic revelations.

In this chapter, the four beasts described correspond to the four parts of the metallic image of chapter two. The lively stone from the mountain is paralleled by an explanation that the kingdoms of men are superseded, once and for all, by the Kingdom of God given to Christ, the Son of Man. We can chart this as follows.

Chapter 2	Chapter 7	Interpretation
Head of Gold	Lion	Babylon
Chest of Silver	Bear	Medo Persia
Belly/Thighs of Brass	Leopard	Greece
Legs/Feet of Iron/Clay	Monstrous Beast	Rome
Stone	Son of Man	God's Empire

Again, in chapter seven, each symbolic vision is appropriate to what it represents. At Babylon, statues of numerous winged lions with human heads have been excavated. The lion was a favorite emblem that ran throughout Babylonian art. It is found on cylinders, statues, in paintings, tiles, etc. This lion, lifted up in pride, was brought down to earth and given a human heart; it was but human after all—its dominion passed away

The bear, raised on one side, signals Persian ascendancy in the Medo-Persian alliance (cf. 8:3, the ram symbol of Persia). Over time, Cyrus made the whole of Media part of the Persian empire. The three ribs in its mouth doubtless stand for the three kingdoms it already had devoured on its way to becoming an empire (probably Egypt, Babylon, and either Assyria or Lydia). More is to be said about this kingdom in chapter eight.

The leopard, Greece, has four wings and four heads, and it moves with great speed—just as Alexander did. The stress on number four speaks of the fourfold division of the empire following Alexander's death. It was divided among his four trusted generals: Cassander, Lysimachus, Seleucus, and Ptolemy. Daniel writes mostly about this third empire for the rest of the book. The concluding chapters focus upon the interactions of the people of God with one of these four parts in particular.

The fourth, nondescript beast is of special concern in chapter seven. Yet no more stress is placed upon it in the rest of the book, since the time when it would hold power was a long way off. But it relates in a big way to the "time of the end," and the book of Revelation picks up where Daniel's message leaves off, to continue in depth the story of the fourth and fifth empires.

Problems seem to loom in the interpretation of the symbols for the Roman Empire. Why is it left nameless? Why is the beast so unidentifiable zoologically? Doubtless, it is because Rome was at that time unknown and its character would prove to be unique in ancient history. To picture it as a "worldwide" empire or to name it "Rome" would have been virtually meaningless to Daniel's contemporaries. But the text makes clear that it would be *different* (cf. v. 7). Look at those ten horns! The other empires were under an emperor. In its early days Rome was a republic, ruled by the senate. And perhaps even more to the point in relation to the ten horns, the Roman Empire consisted of ten provinces, each governed by rulers (proconsuls and praetors) who acted like kings. In Revelation 17:12, in fact, the ten horns are said to "receive authority as kings."

As in Daniel chapter seven, the beast in chapters 13 and 17 of Revelation has ten horns, but in John's vision, the creature shares some of the features of the other beasts of Daniel. Again, the satanic unity of the four world empires is displayed.[3] In both books, the ten horns are contemporaneous; no succession of kings is indicated. They each surrender power to the beast and reign with him for "an hour" (a short time). In Revelation, where greater detail is provided, the beast has seven, and then an eighth head. Eventually (Rev. 17:16), the horns turn on the harlot city and devour her.

Back to Daniel chapter seven. There is also a "little horn" (v. 8) that uproots three of the ten. It has eyes and a boastful mouth (v. 20). It makes war on the saints, but is judged (vv. 21, 22). Daniel's little horn seems to be the same as one of the "heads" of Revelation. John's addition of heads to the imagery allows for the giving of more detailed information, to help us identify the horn, head, or beast (as he is variously called). We can more readily place him in line with the rest of the heads—all Roman emperors. In Revelation, he is further identified as the man whose name numbers 666 (13:18). This seems to point rather definitively to Nero Caesar. (See *The Time Is At Hand*, for details on this identification.)

In Daniel's seventh chapter is also to be found, corresponding to the stone that fills the whole earth (ch. 2), a description of the establishment of the fifth empire—the kingdom (or *empire*) of God. This was also treated in *The Time Is At Hand*, pages 126–129, as follows:

> The time of the establishment of this kingdom is specifically given. It is during the days of the ascendancy of the fourth kingdom: "in the days of those kings" (Dan. 2:44). By no ingenious method of interpretation can this be made to mean some yet future date, more than 1,900 years after the fall of the fourth kingdom. To pretend that the Roman Empire continues today is sheer nonsense. There has been no fourth kingdom (empire) for centuries.
>
> The prophecy speaks of the same kingdom that John, Jesus, and Paul announced. It is the kingdom the apostles preached, and the one Revelation depicts as replacing the Roman empire. According to Mark 1:15, Jesus preached that "the time is fulfilled, and the kingdom of God is at hand." If he did not refer to Daniel's promises of this kingdom, to

3 The Christians' code-name "Babylon" is used for Rome in the book of Revelation (cf. 1 Pet. 5:13), an appropriate *tie*, as in the dream image of Daniel 2—a *whole*, with four successive parts.

the fulfillment of what prophecy *did* he refer? There is but one kingdom predicted. If the kingdom of Christ in the present age is not that kingdom—what is? According to Luke 1:33, the kingdom is the same one Daniel promised, for it is likewise called an "everlasting" kingdom. Hebrews 12 also describes the present kingdom as an everlasting one, thus identifying it with Daniel's promised kingdom.

In a very real sense, the Apocalypse could be said to be a commentary upon the kingdom predictions of Daniel. The ten-horned beast of both books unmistakably connects the two prophecies. Revelation seems to be an enlargement upon Daniel's fourth kingdom prophecy and an extension of the promises of the fifth kingdom. It is significant that Daniel said the kingdom would "stand forever." This allows for no subsequent millennial kingdom to supplant it. It is the eternal kingdom *in time*. It is the millennial kingdom that was realized in the days of the fourth (or Roman) empire. World dominion was taken away from the dragon and given to the saints. History accords perfectly with the prediction that they shall "reign with Christ."

Calvin rightly observes that Daniel 7:9-14 pertains to the ascension and coronation of Christ, and not to the second coming. He says:

> "We have shown how this ought properly to be understood of the commencement of the reign of Christ, and ought not to be connected with its final close, as many interpreters force and strain the passage."[4]

The time when Jesus received the kingdom was at his ascension. The judgment which "was set" and the "books" which "were opened" correspond perfectly to the heavenly court scene in Revelation 4-7. Daniel 7:13 and 14 picture Christ coming *to the Father*, not coming to earth. The kingdom he receives is everlasting; it will not pass away, nor will it be destroyed. In Peter's sermon (Acts 2:29-36), the resurrection and ascension of Christ are interpreted as the fulfillment of God's promise to place Christ upon the throne of David. He says,

"Being therefore a prophet, and knowing that God had sworn by an

4 John Calvin, *Commentary on Daniel* (Grand Rapids: Eerdmans, 1948), Vol. II, p. 38. See also p. 23.

oath to him, that of the fruit of his loins, he would set one upon his throne; he, foreseeing this, spake of the resurrection of Christ.... This Jesus did God raise up, whereof we are all witnesses. Let all the house of Israel therefore know assuredly, that God hath made him both Lord and Christ."

This enthronement (also acknowledged in Acts 15) involved receiving the kingdom of God that Daniel predicted.[5]

Verses 21 and 22 of Daniel 7 sound like a page out of the Apocalypse. The persecuting king of the last world dominion is given brief power to prevail over the saints. But at the judgment-coming of the Ancient of Days (not the second coming of Christ) his power ceases, and the saints receive the kingdom instead. The "judgment" of verse 10 is further explained in verse 26, not as the general judgment (having to do with eternal blessing and condemnation), but as the avenging judgment of God on behalf of his suffering saints. This is the same judgment as that mentioned constantly throughout the book of Revelation. It is defined in verse 26 as taking away dominion from the world power.

This again is in complete agreement with what we have seen in Revelation. Daniel, then, agrees with Revelation: they both teach that the world power will fall in the days of Rome; that God will set up a fifth kingdom with Christ as its ruler; that this kingdom will be world-wide, and consist of the saints of God on earth. For an excellent commentary on the seventh chapter of Daniel in particular, or the book of Daniel in general, none can be commended more highly than Calvin's.

5 Passages like 1 Peter 3:22; Psalm 110:1, and Matthew 28:18, which declare all things subject to Christ, further confirm the fact of His enthronement.

It is of extreme importance, at this juncture, that we stress a point of interpretation we have already mentioned in passing. We cannot emphasize too strongly that the "Son of Man," who in Daniel's vision was "coming with the clouds of heaven," is *not said* to come *to the earth*. Quite to the contrary, He is said to approach the Ancient of Days (7:13). God the Father, to Whom Jesus "comes," is in heaven, not on the earth.

He "comes" (actually returns home) to the heavenly throne. The clouds, associated with the ascension, depict a glorious heavenly scene. THIS IS NOT, therefore, a description of the Second Coming. Those who wrongly consider it to be so, confuse things that expressly differ, and as a result wander far from the true interpretation of the passage.

Note, too, that it is *at this time* (in the days of the Roman kings, at His ascension) that Jesus receives His kingdom according to the verdict of the heavenly court, which has condemned the world empires and stripped them of their dominion. Christ's reception of the eternal empire, in Daniel 7, exactly parallels the coming of the stone that destroys the fourfold metallic image and grows into a world empire that shall never end (cf. the chart on p. 18).

It should be plain that *this* "coming of the Son of Man" is none other than His return to heaven immediately upon His death, resurrection, and victorious ascension, when, in triumph, He lead captivity captive (Ephesians 4:8). It is His "coming" viewed from above, a picture of what transpired on the other side of the cloud that received Him "out of their sight" (Acts 1:9). It is the same event that Jesus predicts in the Olivet discourse, shown below in parallel from the synoptic Gospels:

Matthew 24:30	Mark 13:26	Luke 21:27
And at that time the sign of the Son of Man will appear in heaven...and they will see the Son of Man coming on the clouds of heaven with power and much glory.	And at that time they will see the Son of Man coming in clouds with great power and glory.	The at that time they will see the Son of Man coming on a cloud with great power and glory.

Note especially the parallels with Daniel 7:13-14. In all four places Jesus is called the "Son of Man." He is said to "come in (or, better, "with") clouds." Third, He is the One Who is given "power and glory." (See Matt. 26:62-65, Jesus' words to Caiaphas.)

Next, we see the gathering of the elect from all the earth (Matt. 24:31; Mark 13:27) and the redemption of the saints (Luke 21:28), in the succeeding verses, respectively. Thus, two seemingly distinct concepts are actually paralleled in the three passages. Do not Luke's "redemption" and the gathering of the saints by the messengers (the meaning of the word angels") of Christ find their harmony in the words of Daniel? Chapter seven, verse 18 reads, "but the saints of the Most High will receive the kingdom and will possess the kingdom forever—even for all eternity;" and in verses 21-22, 25-27, the persecution of the saints is predicted, followed by the judgment of the fourth beast and the handing over of the kingdom (empire) "under the whole heaven" to the saints. The drawing near of redemption and the gathering of the elect "from one end of the heaven to the other" ties the two concepts together. The saints are rescued *from persecution*, a theme struck early in the Olivet discourse. The preaching of the gospel in all the world, as Christ's messengers go forth to gather the elect from the "uttermost parts," the "four winds," and from "under the whole heaven," is clear evidence of this gathering.

The Olivet Discourse continues with the parable of the fig tree. The point of this parable, as Matthew and Mark clearly say, is that "when you see these things happening, know that He is near, at the door." Or, as Luke puts it, "know that the kingdom of God is near." Again, the parallelism here indicates that when Christ's kingdom comes, He comes. First He comes to the Father to receive the kingdom, then He comes to His church by the Holy Spirit into this kingdom.

All these events took place in that generation in which the Gospel writers wrote. (See Matthew 24:34; Mark 13:30, and Luke 21:32, where Jesus speaks plainly of "this generation.") It is as Daniel had declared when he announced the coming of the kingdom "in the days of those (the Roman) kings." Not all "comings" (as demonstrated in *The Time Is At Hand*) refer to the second coming of Christ (for which we look, but which is but one very important coming), just as not all "ends" refer to the end of our New Testament era; a number of occurrences refer, rather, to the end of the Old Testament age or "economy."

You may be hesitant to accept this (perhaps it is new to you) interpretation of the Olivet Discourse. But do not turn aside from the understanding of Daniel 7 as the ascension scene, simply on that account. This understanding, rightly adopted by Calvin and others, is crucial to the proper interpretation of Daniel's overall prophecy. Whatever views you now hold regarding Matthew 24 and Luke 21, the interpretation of Daniel 7 stands on its own. At the same time, starting out with a clear picture of what God had already revealed through His servant Daniel throws a great deal of light on the eschatology of the New Testament.

We have discussed these issues at length simply because they are so central, so basic, and so important in biblical prophecy. We shall view chapter seven again, in its regular order, below.

Chapter 3
The Angel in the Fire

In chapter one, we saw how Daniel was able to circumvent a direct confrontation about Babylonian food and drink. But, as the apostles and many of the prophets had found, it isn't always possible to do that. Sometimes it becomes necessary to meet social or political demands head-on, for the sake of God's will. That's what Shadrach, Meshach, and Abednego (and later on, Daniel himself) discovered. What makes the difference? How do you know when to say, "We must obey God rather than men" (Acts 5:29)? We shall investigate that important question in a moment. First, consider the story.

Prodded by some unscrupulous informers, and jealous of their place in Nebuchadnezzar's government, some officials aroused the king's anger against Shadrach, Meshach, and Abednego. They had refused to bow before the gold colossus[1] he had erected in the plain of Dura. He summoned them before him and, to his credit, checked out the facts (vv. 13-15). He gave them the opportunity either to refute the charges or to comply with the original order, but from their own mouths he heard their self-condemning words.

The three young men admitted they had not bowed before the golden image, and they offered neither an excuse nor any extenuating circumstances that might explain their actions. It was a simple matter of their refusing to worship any other god than Jehovah God (vv. 16–18). Moreover, they used this opportunity to give clear testimony to the lordship of Jehovah in all nations and over all things, saying,

> *If that happens, our God, Whom we serve, is able to deliver us from the blazing oven fire, so He will deliver us from your hand, O King. But if*

1 A colossus is any statue larger than life-size.

> *not, let it be known to you, O King, that we are not going to serve your gods, nor will we worship the image of gold you have set up.*
> (vv. 17-18)

Their testimony was clear and unambiguous. It was a respectful but direct reply to the challenge Nebuchadnezzar had issued when he asked them, "Then who is the god who shall deliver you out of my hands?" (end of v. 15.)

When does one refuse to obey the government? The principle is plain. Whenever God's people are *required* to disobey God *in order to* obey the government, they *must* refuse. In other words, they must be ordered, as were Shadrach, Meshach, and Abednego, to violate a clear commandment of God—in this case, the command not to bow down to any idol.

Governments, churches, homes, and businesses are examples of authority/submission structures described in the Bible. To each realm God has assigned certain authority. But it is in each case a limited authority, appropriate to that particular sphere. The authority specifically delegated to each cannot be appropriated by another without serious consequences. Whenever that does happen, the people of God are in difficult circumstances.

In Romans 13, the authority of the sword is said to be given to the ruler, to exercise God's vengeance (v. 4). In Romans 12, individuals (serving in any other capacity) are forbidden to take vengeance (12:19), but are instead told to overcome evil with good (12:21).

We have already made reference to Acts 5, in which the state forbade the apostles from preaching in the name of Jesus. Their reply, "We must obey God rather than men," is carefully worded. Note that it is not a matter of the authority God gave to the state being in conflict with that given to the church. God gives no authority in one sphere that would clash with the authority He delegates to another. That would make Him a God of confusion (See 1 Cor. 14:33). The apostles' statement contrasts the authority of *God* with the authority of *men*. The state, which had no authority to forbid preaching, had exceeded its God-given mandate and acted purely on arrogated human authority. That's why the apostles said they would not obey "men." God allows no authority that would require anyone to commit sin.

The case at hand, of Shadrach, Meshach, and Abednego, was a pagan usurpation of authority. The king had set himself in the place of God, demanding from his subjects such worship as he dictated. He had no authority to do so. Such a command was in itself a challenge to the true God. That is why the three Hebrews, with a perfect right to do so, refused to obey.

What can we say, then, about the precise circumstances under which one may (must) disobey the government? Look at those that seem clear from this event. When you are called on the carpet about a matter of your faith, you are required to stand fast for the truth. If you are unable to convince the authorities to exclude you from the command, you are required to disobey. The command issued by the government must be one that *requires* you to disobey God. Earlier, Daniel and his three young companions had been able to avoid a direct confrontation because the circumstances were different. An alternative was possible and did become available. Here, a public decree had been issued requiring everyone to bow before the image. It was not a private matter. In addition, there was a direct, public challenge to God Himself: "Then who is the god who shall deliver you out of my hands?" (v. 15). In his excessive pride, Nebuchadnezzar pitted his personal power (note the words, "*my* hands"), not even that of his gods, against the power of the almighty God! These, then, are some of the elements that force one to stand firm and to refuse to obey.

Politely refusing even under pressure, the three gave no defense for the charge against them (vv. 16-17). In effect, they pleaded guilty. And they remained firm. Moreover, in that tense situation, they gave ringing testimony to the God Whom they served. Their words were in direct contradiction to the proud challenge. They said, in effect: You ask which God can deliver us from your hand? We'll tell you. Jehovah, our God, is able to deliver us (v. 17).

They were careful, however, not to *presume* that God would deliver them. They laid no demand upon God: "But even if He does not …" (v. 18). God *could* deliver them, they affirmed; that He *would*, they would not predict. Sometimes He does deliver from persecution and trial (ch. 1); and sometimes He delivers out of it (ch. 3 and 5). For all they knew, He might remove them from the hands of the king by means of their death. Other prophets had died for their faith and loyalty to God. In any event, God would deliver them from compromise arising from fear of death.

What was the outcome of this dramatic crisis? In the end, God's reputation, as the God of providence, was honored through their rescue. Representatives from many nations had gathered for the festival. They all had to admit that Jehovah was everything that Shadrach, Meshach, and Abednego had claimed (v. 27). And Nebuchadnezzar himself, who had so proudly challenged God, was forced by the turn of events to back down and acknowledge Jehovah (vv. 28ff.).

What of that "fourth person" walking in the fire (v. 25)? Who was he? The king said he looked like a "son of the gods." Consider that this expression fell from the lips of a pagan king engrossed in idolatry, a man who, in such a situation, hardly knew how to express himself. The text explicitly calls the rescuer an "angel" (v. 28), as it does also in Daniel 6:22, in the later deliverance from the lion's den. Whether *this* angel (the word signifies "messenger") was *the* "Angel of the Covenant" Who appeared to the patriarchs and others, and Whom many take to be Jesus in pre-incarnation appearances, is not certain. Angels elsewhere in the book of Daniel are distinguished from Him. So here the question is moot; it cannot be answered with any certainty. One thing is sure. Three men were cast into the top opening of the smelting furnace and three men emerged from the bottom of it. But during the ordeal itself, four were counted. Just when needed, God's messenger was there, protecting and encouraging.

Could not God have saved them without an angel? Of course. But the presence of the angel, visible in the fire, confirmed to these unbelievers that Jehovah had directly intervened. The unscorched clothing, without even the smell of fire on it, also gave evidence that this was a divine miracle, and not a fluke of some sort.

The world erects its golden images today. And it heats up its blazing furnaces to intimidate those who refuse to bow to them. Public opinion, polled majorities, vocal minorities, money, fame—all these in one way or another put pressure on God's servants, seeking to make them conform to sinful behavior. We have our modern Chaldeans everywhere, who delight in reporting when Christians refuse to bow. So this account is intended to encourage believers today, as in all ages, not to bend the knee to these gods. Our God does not want you to buckle when faced with the fiery furnaces of criticism, ostracism, or deprivation.

To mention but one sad example, we find it in some churches. There are ineffective, unbelieving "Magi" occupying the pulpits of stolen churches, built by their believing forefathers. They want the true pastors, who still worship the God of Heaven, to renege on their convictions, water down their doctrine and message, and become like them—or they will have them thrown into the fire.

The Colossus of Gold

Critics with faulty knowledge of ancient times and ways, but with the intention of shaking people's faith in the Bible, have scoffed at the details given in chapter three of Daniel, calling it a highly imaginative fable. In particular, they've poked fun at the idea of a golden image ninety to a hundred and five feet tall. "Incredible!" they say. Is this truly beyond belief?

Colossi are known to have existed in ancient civilizations. The Greeks produced many, of which the Colossus of Rhodes (of bronze, 105-112 feet high) is the most famous. It was declared one of the seven wonders of the ancient world. Over a hundred colossi were reported to be on the island of Rhodes alone. Another of the seven wonders was a colossus of Zeus at Olympus, forty feet tall and made of (at least embellished with) gold and ivory.

The colossus of Nero was 110-120 feet high. Hadrian had to employ twenty-four elephants to drag it away. A colossus of Rameses II, seen by Nebuchadnezzar, was a hundred feet high. To get a modern perspective on all this, note that the Statue of Liberty stands 152 feet tall, on a pedestal 150 feet high.

Everything Nebuchadnezzar did was colossal. One needs only to think of the hanging gardens and of the great walls of Babylon (300 feet high; 75 feet thick, and composed of 18,750 million of Babylon's largest bricks!)—unsurpassed in that part of the world.

But why so much gold for such a statue? The statue could have been hollow (like the Statue of Liberty), or another material could have been overlaid, or "plated," with gold. Isaiah 40:19 refers to this as common practice. Oh well, perhaps scholars cooped up in tiny rooms, supported by small seminary or university budgets, can be excused for thinking small!

Then too, do you wonder where Daniel was during this episode? The answer is simple. We do not know. Perhaps he was away on a state mission. Or perhaps the conspirators were afraid to touch him, because he was too high in the government and in the personal favor of the king. We just don't know. But apparently he was not involved directly in this particular challenge, or he too would have been cast into the furnace.

Chapter 4
The Second Dream and the King's Edict

"When will you ever learn?" The words could be those of your own mother when you were small. Or they could have been addressed to Pharaoh in Egypt by Moses, or to Nebuchadnezzar by Daniel in Babylon. Again and again Nebuchadnezzar had to be taught the same lesson. But, as with Pharaoh, ultimately something drastic had to be done to make it sink in.

This is the account of how God finally brought this pagan king to an acknowledgment of His sovereignty. At best, all his previous declarations about the "god of heaven" had been assertions of a pagan mind: that Jehovah was a great god among the gods.

When his humiliating experience came to an end, Nebuchadnezzar issued an imperial edict in the form of an official state paper. Assyriologists have unearthed many such ancient edicts, but none with a content even beginning to approximate this one. History records few if any imperial dreams or maladies, certainly not one preserved as a formal edict from a head of state. The Bible narrates events in the lives of patriarchs and rulers that may seem to parallel this, but here we have an official governmental proclamation. Nothing quite like this has been found among the Jews, Greeks, or Romans.

We do know that the Mesopotamians left records of this sort, for we have discovered state "papers" of a similar format from Assurbanipal of Assyria and Nabonidus of Babylon. In the case of this particular edict, it is accurate not only in its formal details, but also in its style. The remarkable thing about this edict, however, is not simply its frankness (rulers usually "doctored up" the facts to make themselves look good), but that it contains a confession of faith in Jehovah, the God of Israel (vv. 2-3).

The dream about a great tree that was felled and sprouted again—fulfilled in the life of Nebuchadnezzar, who went mad for seven years but recovered when he repented of his self-aggrandizement (4:27, 34, 37)—is what God used to lead the king to an acknowledgment of His sovereignty. The entire experience was designed and intended to do just that.

Nebuchadnezzar had already come to know something of God's work and power through the fiery furnace episode of chapter three and Daniel's revelation of the dream of the metallic image and its meaning in chapter two. But, like so many of us, he simply forgot the lesson and went on with his life. It is rather obvious that he never considered the claims of the true God on his personal life. Now, in chapter four, we have another dream, along with Daniel's interpretation and application of it to the king himself. Daniel urged the king to acknowledge that God was indeed sovereign over the kingdoms of men, that He alone controlled world history (4:25). The prophet suggested that Nebuchadnezzar would avoid the tragedy foreseen in the dream by repentance and the amending of his ways (4:27); but he still didn't listen—though God gave him a full year to repent (4:29).

Instead, walking the rooftop of his grand palace, he uttered the proud boast,

> *Is not this that Great Babylon that I have built, as the palace of my realm, by my mighty power and for the splendor of my majesty?*
>
> (v. 30)

Even as these words fell from his lips (v. 31), the lightning struck the tree! From heaven above, God pronounced judgment in an audible voice (vv. 31-32), and Nebuchadnezzar was stricken with madness. He remained in that condition for seven years, until he acknowledged that Jehovah God, not he, was sovereign (v. 32^{b}).

It is noteworthy that the official edict cited in this chapter of Daniel may be the only instance in the world's history of such a formal confession of Israel's God prior to the coming of Christ. Some Christian rulers have done so in our era, to be sure. The crucial factor is this: God was confessed as sovereign; this is the key issue in Daniel's book.

What can we say about Nebuchadnezzar's madness? His disease, called "lycanthropy" because the one afflicted imagines himself to be a wolf, was rather widely recognized in ancient times. Galen mentions it along with other delusions. It is reported that among the Dead Sea fragments was found a prayer for Nabonidus, the last king of Babylon (father of Belshazzar), who is said to have suffered an illness for seven years. Speculations abound concerning Nebuchadnezzar's ailment. But one thing is certain: it was a direct judgment from God and needs no other explanation. Apparently he had lucid periods since, at length, upon reflection, he did realize what had happened to him, and he repented.

What happened to the government of Babylon during those seven years? The king was obviously "out of it." Things went right on, as did the governments of France, Denmark, England, and Bavaria when Charles IV, Christian VII, George III, and Otho, respectively, went mad.

God brought down mighty Nebuchadnezzar for his pride. Think of it! The grand emperor of Babylon crawling around on the ground, trying to eat grass like an ox. His hair grew wild and his nails grew long like the talons of an eagle. Truly, pride precedes a fall! But it was, ultimately, only through such an experience—avoidable as it was, had he changed his ways during the twelve months extended to him—that he accepted what it seemed he would never learn. God has His ways of bringing not only rulers, but all proud people, to bow humbly before His throne. Either now, by humble submission and faith, or later, in condemnation *by force*, all will confess Him to be the sovereign and only God of the universe.

Heavenly Spectator Participants

We do not need to wait for Daniel's accounts of his visions, recorded in the second half of his book, to read of the part angels play in his life and service for God. In fact, in the previous chapter we heard about a fourth personage walking in the furnace with the three Israelites, described by Nebuchadnezzar as both a "son of the gods" and an "angel" (3:25, 28). Now, in chapter four, we learn of "watchers" (literally "wakeful ones"), "holy ones" (vv. 13, 17). Although "and" connects the two terms in the Aramaic text, we can take this in the sense of "even" or "that is," a double description of a single entity (4:13).

We have here a glimpse into something that can only excite, without satisfying, our curiosity. We are made aware of the apparent cognizance of, and even a degree of participation in, things transpiring in human history on the part of supramundane beings. Other passages such as Luke 15:7, 10; 1 Cor. 11:10, and Eph. 3:10 imply the same thing.

The epistle to the Hebrews speaks more specifically to our Daniel passage. As he related his dream to Daniel, Nebuchadnezzar told how the angel (holy watcher) spoke, within the action of the dream (4:14-17). As part of that utterance came the declaration, "The sentence is by decision of the watchers, and the decree from the word of the holy ones" (v. 17). That is where the epistle to the Hebrews sheds some light on the role of angels in divine revelation. First we have a general statement, formed as a question: "Aren't they all ministering spirits sent off to serve for the benefit of those who are going to inherit salvation?" (Heb. 1:14). Then this: "If the word spoken through angels was certain … how can we escape if we neglect such a great salvation?" (2:2, 3). The original allusion to angelic mediation of the Ten Commandments to Moses is found, not in his narrative report in Exodus, but in Moses' final blessing upon the Israelites. In Deuteronomy 33:2 we read, "He came from Sinai with a holy myriad (ten thousands of holy ones) … [with] a fiery law[2] for them." This shows us the reserve with which Scripture deals with such extraterrestrial or supramundane intrusions into the affairs of earthly history.

Human history, then, is for heavenly beings (and conceivably other creatures within this massive universe) a grand drama, in which they express great interest. Peter, in his first letter, speaks of the longing of the Old Testament prophets to comprehend their own inspired predictions about the sufferings and glories of the Messiah. Then he explains that these were the things now expounded in the New Testament, the gospel (good news) of redemption in Christ, "things that the angels desire to look into" (1 Peter 1:12).

This is not a drama in which you and I are merely play actors. It is real life. It reminds one of the Civil War when crowds gathered on the

2 Some alternate meanings for this Aramaic term have been suggested such as "a flaming fire" (RSV), "flashing lightning" (NASB), "[from his] mountain slopes" (NIV), and "streaming along" (NEB).

hillsides—not to watch a play, but the real thing! It is a drama where the course of history unfolds, as if being viewed on live TV. So as they watch, they recognize that it was Nebuchadnezzar and other kings who are brought to see: God is the main participant in this drama. The war between Satan's world kingdoms and the people of the kingdom of God progresses through the ages until the downfall of world dominion with the death and resurrection of Jesus Christ, whereby "all authority in heaven and on earth has been given" to Him. (Matt. 28:18; Dan. 2:44. Compare also Dan. 7:13-14, 26-27, describing His ascension and enthronement.)

In all of this, God is purposefully exhibiting His sovereign nature, pouring out wrath or mercy as it befits each occasion. The Apostle Paul declares, in his penetrating epistle to the Romans, "What if God, wishing to demonstrate His wrath and to make known His power, endured with great patience the vases of wrath designed for destruction, in order to make known the riches of His glory toward the vases of mercy, that He designed beforehand for glory …" (Rom. 9:22-23).

If the book of Daniel demonstrates anything, it is that there is more to history than meets the eye. There is much activity going on in the unseen world, and that activity has its effect on what transpires in this world. As the book of Job so clearly shows, the human drama is to a great extent the playing out of a heavenly history with which it is inextricably intertwined (additional insight is found in Eph. 6:12 and Rev. 12:7-12).

While the curtain is but slightly drawn aside, and that for only a brief moment, Daniel—perhaps supremely among biblical books gives us the clearest picture not only of the reality of heavenly activity but also of the effect it has on human history. As we move on, we will note how this is true elsewhere in the book.

Chapter 5
God Crashes the Party

The narrative in this chapter falls into four parts:

1. Background and setting (vv. 1-4)
2. The handwriting on the wall (vv. 5-16)
3. Daniel's words of rebuke (vv. 17-23)
4. The interpretation and its fulfillment (vv. 24-31)

For years the critics pounced upon Daniel five as evidence of historical blunders in sacred Scripture. The Bible here presents Belshazzar as the last king of the Babylonian Empire. Yet extrabiblical sources, such as Greek historians, named Nabonidus as the last. Moreover, these sources placed him at the fortress of Borsippa and declared that Cyrus allowed him to live. Worse yet, there was no trace of a king named Belshazzar outside of the Bible, and no place in the list of kings for him. So strong were these attacks that one defender of the scriptural record called his book *Daniel in the Critics' Den.*

The solution to these concerns is one of the most thrilling stories in the annals of modern archaeology. The spade has dug up evidence to clarify the historical situation and thus vindicate the biblical account. The critics were muzzled on this one.

Here's the story. In 1858, Henry Rawlinson found a terra cotta cylinder at Ur of the Chaldees, and it mentioned Belshazzar, as the eldest son of Nabonidus. Later on, an account of Babylon's capture was also found. This record indicates that Nabonidus had left the capital prior to the attack, but that "the king died." It mentions that the city was taken at night, just as Daniel says (5:30-31). Further investigation of all available archaeological evidence indicated that Nabonidus had indeed appointed Belshazzar as co-regent during the latter part of his reign. New light is thrown, in turn, on another aspect of this account. It appears that Belshazzar's offer to make Daniel the "third ruler" (Dan. 5:16, 20) was in fact his proposal to form a triumvirate—Daniel together with his father Nabonidus and himself. It was not an option to establish Daniel as *second* only to himself, as in the case of Joseph to the pharaoh.

So then, quite contrary to all the aspersions cast upon the Bible's record of these events, such details provide strong evidence of their factual historicity. In so complex a situation, who but a contemporary would have had before him the information about this triumvirate? Someone writing fiction many years later, as critics have claimed, would hardly create this incidental detail from his own imagination.

Furthermore, it has been asserted that the passage is in error because Belshazzar is said to be the son of Nebuchadnezzar (vv. 11, 18). Though we have insufficient information to certify the exact relationship, more than one option is opened to us by the fact that in Arabic usage (and as likely in the Babylonian Akkadian) the term "father" has seven distinct uses, and "son" even more. The "queen" who speaks here may have been the queen mother, in fact, a widow of Nebuchadnezzar, and possibly also the wife of Nabonidus. Belshazzar could have been Nebuchadnezzar's grandson, or even a direct son adopted by Nabonidus, the usurper of the throne. With several possibilities available, one ought not reject outright the statement of the Bible. A receptive attitude is right, whether out of a wholesome reverence for the Scriptures or as a sensible precaution against being proved wrong by future discovery (as so often has happened). There is no confusion here, except in the minds of those who are predisposed to find inaccuracies in the Bible.

That's not all. It was predicted nearly two hundred years earlier (Isaiah 45:1-2) that Cyrus (called *by name*) would open Babylon's double gates and cut its bars of iron. The way in which Cyrus conquered Babylon was remarkable. The city was considered impregnable. The Medo-Persian army began to invade about two years prior to the events recorded in Daniel 5. The city was then surrounded. Yet Belshazzar remained unperturbed. The Euphrates River flowed right through Babylon, providing an unfailing water supply. There were stores laid up to withstand a siege of ten years or more. Farms within the city's walls could provide fresh food. Those walls, perhaps 300 feet high and 75 feet thick, made the city impregnable—or so Belshazzar thought. Why worry about Cyrus and his army? Why not carry on with his drunken orgies?

But Cyrus did find a way into the city. He dug great ditches and, the very night described for us in Daniel five, by literally diverting the entire Euphrates River, he and his men marched under the wall by way of the river bed! Though there were also walls along the river inside the city, gates in these were commonly left unlocked. So Cyrus opened the gates and took the city as prophesied. Belshazzar, as reported by Daniel, was slain that same night.

Now it is clear why the book of Daniel mentions at the very outset how the vessels of the temple were carried off (1:2). It is from these very vessels that Belshazzar and some of his thousand guests were drinking during this fateful feast. In the telling of Babylon's story as to its connection with the people of God, at both the beginning and end, these sacred vessels figure prominently. They tie the story together as with a ribbon.

We read that Belshazzar drank in the presence of his guests (v. 1). This is strange, since the king's table was usually set in private, apart from the others and screened off. But not this night. This was to be a public orgy. Women were present (v. 2), and the wine flowed freely. It was in this setting that Belshazzar, in defiance of God and with arrogant sacrilege, ordered that the vessels of the temple of Jerusalem be brought for them to drink from. As they drank, they "praised the gods of gold and silver, of bronze, iron, wood, and stone" (v. 4).

What brazen, shameless idolatry! God would not allow His matchless name thus to be sullied. Suddenly, high up on the wall, on the white plaster above the brick, something began to appear. All in the chamber could now see a hand—like the hand of a man—writing something on the surface. It wrote the words: "MENE, MENE, TEKEL, and PHARSIN." What did those words mean?

The king became so frightened that his pale face froze into a ghastly stare; his knees knocked together, his legs grew limp (v. 6). Even in his inebriated state, he was doubtless aware this was a message of judgment, sent from the God he had just blatantly insulted.

What was that message? He had to find out at once. Belshazzar was fully aware of all that the God of heaven had done in the days of King Nebuchadnezzar (vv. 18-24). Still, he had defiantly blasphemed Him by toasting inanimate gods, out of the very vessels that belonged to the true

God of Israel. He did not act out of ignorance. He gave affront to Almighty God. Response was immediate and terrifying! In the face of such behavior, God did not remain silent. He took immediate and definitive action. This was the time and place for God to show the entire civilized world of that day (and to all succeeding generations through His Word) that He is the sovereign God of all.

Why doesn't God respond like this when a Voltaire or an Ingersoll shakes his fist heavenward and dares God to strike him? It is important to answer this question. First, it is unnecessary. Once God has spoken and placed it in His written Word for posterity, He need not condescend to repeat Himself. Second, God does not obey the directions of men—especially those who oppose Him. Here, He was acting according to His own program. He was declaring His sovereignty to the world rulers who would anticipate the coming of His Son, the King of kings (cf. 5:21[b], 5:23[b]). In his day Nebuchadnezzar had but little light, and God was patient with him. Belshazzar had more, and was judged for his deliberate and defiant blasphemy.

Writing on the wall by a hand unattached to a body?! It was plain with Whom Belshazzar was dealing. God had prepared the way, so there could be no mistake about the supernatural origin of the phenomenon. God had earlier sent that fourth person to appear in the fire, and He had spoken in a voice from heaven to the pagan king Nebuchadnezzar—a rare occurrence. Then, a detached hand wrote on the wall. God did not even need to send a hand to inscribe the words. But the high drama of the moment, the attention-grabbing feature that lent to the impact of the supernatural, was the presence of the fingers which moved across the wall. The divine message was:

MENE, MENE	"Numbered, numbered," signifying the empire had come to an end. Belshazzar's days had been numbered and his "number was up!"
TEKEL	"Weighed," reporting that he had been placed on God's scales and he had been found lacking, no longer fit to be king.
PHARSIN	"Divided, shattered," indicating that his empire was about to be destroyed.

Babylon's astrologers could see the words, but were unable to explain their significance. Only Daniel could. The king had promised a high reward, but Daniel refused it in advance (v. 17). Why? For good reason. Though he had already accepted other positions he had been offered, this time two things determined his resolve not to. Not only would acceptance be meaningless since the empire would fall that very night, but Daniel also refused to serve a king who had knowingly blasphemed his God. Nebuchadnezzar, whom he had served so faithfully, was of a different sort. He both acknowledged the God of Israel (ch. 2) and humbled himself before Him (ch. 4). There are some unsaved persons with or for whom Christians may work, but there are also those whom they should not accommodate. There was hope for Nebuchadnezzar, but none for Belshazzar.

The Queen Mother remembered Daniel favorably. The king proceeded with his high appointment, with special symbols of royalty, probably over Daniel's protest (v. 29). But all flattery aside, God's servant admonished the king boldly just prior to his reading of the divine message (vv. 18-24). He contrasted Belshazzar with Nebuchadnezzar, recalling God's miraculous dealings with the latter, all well known to Belshazzar—"in spite of your full awareness" (v. 22). This even included Nebuchadnezzar's personal confession of God's sovereignty (v. 21).

Note how in verse 23 Daniel labels the sinful ruler's actions for what they were: *rebellion* against God ("you have risen up against the Lord of Heaven"), *sacrilege* ("the vessels of His house you had brought before you, and you and your nobles and your consorts have drunk wine from them"), *idolatry* ("the senseless gods of silver and gold ... you have praised"), and *slight* ("and the God in Whose hand is your breath and all your ways you have failed to honor.") Belshazzar dishonored God, and for that he was destroyed. He had failed to acknowledge not only that his power and authority was subject to the God of the Bible, but also that God held his very life in His hand.

When Cyrus took the city, he placed its rule into the hands of one "Darius the Mede" (v. 31), a personage whose identity has been variously described by biblical scholars and historians. He figures prominently in the next chapter, the last of the narrative series in this book. Verse 31 is thus a transitional one, anticipating the dramatic story of chapter six.

Chapter 6
God's Angel in the Den

Chapter five concluded the account of God's dealings with the Babylonian world-empire in its relation to His people. It tied in well with the story begun in the second verse of chapter one, the story of how the vessels from the temple in Jerusalem were carried off at the time Daniel and his friends were deported.

Some time had now elapsed. We don't know how much, but perhaps as little as two years. Darius, placed on the throne of Babylon by Cyrus, a follower of the religion of Zoroaster, was sixty-two years of age at the time (5:31). Daniel, now that man's senior by about twenty years, retained a position of recognized authority and prominence. If anything, with this change of rule from Babylonian to Medo-Persian, his fame seems to have grown. He answered directly to the king, and under him were at least forty satraps of the province of Babylon. He acquitted himself well and was so well liked by Darius that word was abroad that the king was planning to elevate him to a position as his right-hand man.

This contemplated promotion incited the envy of the other officials, themselves jealous for the position and resentful of this foreigner's rise to such a place of power (v. 13 indicates ethnic resentment). So they plotted to *get* Daniel. Personally acquainted with graft and other of forms of corruption routinely committed by those in high places, they scoured Daniel's records for evidence. To their surprise, they found none; his record was spotless (v. 4). Incensed by their failure, they plotted the one and only way to trap him. They'd get at him through his known religious commitment and practices.

Consider for a moment Daniel's clean record. How few there are in politics (or in business) of whom it can be said, "If we're going to get him, it will have to come from his faithful service to God." Were someone to scrutinize *your* record for negligence or corruption, what would he find? You needn't be a politician, where such faults are more the rule than the exception. Even as an employee, business person, or homemaker, how do you measure up? How about those tax returns? Could you stand the test of the investigative reporter out to dig up dirt?

So these antagonists devised a diabolical plan, calculating on its appeal to the king's vanity, and at the same time either forcing Daniel to deny his faith or walk straight into their trap. (Notice how Daniel does not actively provoke antagonism or persecution; he merely continues doing the right thing.) We all know the story, recounted by Daniel himself:

> *Then these high officials and satraps banded themselves together hurriedly before the king and spoke thus to him: King Darius, Live forever! All the royal officials, prefects, satraps, advisers, and pashas have taken counsel together, that the king should issue a decree which ratifies a prohibition: Anyone who prays a petition from any god or man, up to thirty days, except of you, O King, let him be thrown into the lions' pit. Now, O King, Let the prohibition be issued and sign the writing, that it cannot be altered, according to the law of the Medes and Persians which cannot be abolished. Thereupon, King Darius signed the inscribed prohibition.*
>
> (Daniel 6:6-9, vv. 7-10 in Aramaic text)

Thus reassured, this murderous mob spied on Daniel as he prayed in his accustomed manner. They then returned to King Darius, and, reminding him of the binding nature of his decree, they "squealed" on Daniel, the Jewish exile whom they despised (v. 13). At once the king realized that this law, which they had so deviously proposed, was not designed to be obeyed, but to be broken—by Daniel!

Again, Daniel's own words recounting this treacherous behavior of supposedly trustworthy civil servants paint the circumstances in vivid hues:

> *As for Daniel, though he knew that the decree was written, he went up to his house and, with windows in his upper chamber opened toward Jerusalem, three times a day he knelt down and prayed and gave thanks*

> *before his God, just as he had done previously. Then those same men ganged up and found Daniel; he was praying and making intercession before his God. Next, they approached and spoke before the king concerning the king's decree: Did you not sign a decree, that any man who prays of any god or man besides you for thirty days, O King, he shall be thrown into the lions' pit? The king answered and said, The edict stands, in accordance with the law of the Medes and Persians, which cannot be abolished. Thereupon they responded, saying to the king, that Daniel, who is of the Jewish exiles, fails to have regard for you, O King, or for the decree which you have signed; but three times a day he says his prayers.*
>
> (Dan. 6:10-13, vv. 11-14 in Aramaic text)

Thus, Daniel knew very well the consequences of praying toward Jerusalem with open windows, in conscious defiance of the king's command. "Why, then, did he leave the windows open?" you ask. In this particular situation he could have closed the shutters, though they generally sat open because of the heat. Certainly he was not out to display his "rebellion" from sheer defiance. He had no reason or intention to arouse anger unnecessarily. Nor was his manner one of pietistic bravado. "Why, then?"

There are at least two reasons that probably entered his thinking. First of all, to abandon or even modify his regular practice would have amounted to a denial, or at least a weakening, of his faith in and testimony to Jehovah, the Sovereign God. It would have shown that out of fear of men he had dishonored God, in the very presence of a godless enemy. On the other hand, had he managed to conceal his practice, these adversaries would have asked him why he had abandoned his usual custom in the face of this new edict. Daniel would have either been forced to lie, which they well knew he wouldn't do, or would have to confess the truth to his own destruction.

Back to King Darius. He was utterly shattered! He'd been tricked by deceitful men, Daniel's inferiors, and he knew it. By allowing himself to be swept along by their appeal to his vanity (the decree implied his superiority to all gods, if only for the thirty days), he had acted foolishly.

It was at the same time against his own best interest. Daniel was a valuable adviser and administrator whom he could ill afford to lose; besides, he thought warmly of Daniel (note vv. 14, 16, 18-20).

Still, there was no way open for him to rescue Daniel. The irrevocable nature of the laws of the Medes and Persians (v. 15) were designed in the first place to force kings to think twice before issuing a decree, thus to avoid making this very sort of mistake. In the end, Darius himself was forced to confess that reliance upon Jehovah was the only hope. So he meekly encouraged Daniel, who had already been thrown to the lions, "Your God, Whom you constantly serve, He will rescue you" (v. 16[b]). How this proud king had been brought low!

Early the next morning, after a sleepless night, the king was at the lions' pit. The seals were still intact and the stone in place. No one could have tampered with anything, yet Daniel was safe and sound. An angel from the Lord appeared, says Daniel, and "shut the lions' mouths." Note the careful detail provided in the account of just what took place in verse 17. The pit was covered over and sealed, not just with the signet ring imprint of the king, but by others as well. Any intervention (by an angel, for instance, as Daniel tells us) had to be the work of God.

Those evil fellows who so cleverly trapped Daniel were themselves, together with their families (in a practice explicitly forbidden by Mosaic law: Deut. 24:16; 2 Kings 14:6), thrown to the lions.[3] In addition, Darius, acting more like Nebuchadnezzar than like Belshazzar, sent out a decree to all people in the Medo-Persian Empire to revere the living God of Daniel in open acknowledgment of His sole possession of the power to save (vv. 26-27).

How Satan, the energizer of these world empires (cf. ch. 2), must have bristled at this defeat of his purposes! Above all, he must have cringed at seeing his own servants proclaiming the praises of the true God, as the outcome of Jehovah's overruling of the most carefully laid plans of his diabolical design. Here, by the king's decree, his puppet captains were going over to his Enemy!

---

3 Why were they not thrown into a fiery furnace, as were Daniel's companions? Fire was sacred to Zoroastrians; so, unlike the Babylonians, they employed lions for executions. This detail again shows the careful authenticity of the text.

The major point is that, in the grand demonstration of God's power and grace set forth in the book of Daniel, we see kings and kingdoms being subdued, brought to their knees before Him. As for Daniel, he continued to prosper throughout the rest of Darius' local rule and on into the longer and wider reign of Emperor Cyrus.

Chapter 7
The Ascension and Session of Christ

We now enter the truly "prophetic" section of Daniel's book, the *predictive* material. This follows quite logically after his accounts of personal dealings with the kings of the satanic world empires. As we've already seen, the initial vision given to Daniel in chapter seven parallels the emperor's dream in chapter two. But this chapter adds much by way of expansion. It also provides a transition to that second Hebrew portion of the text, which begins with chapter eight and runs to the end of the book.

In the Introduction we saw that the Hebrew parts of Daniel's book are directed principally to God's own people. It is therefore highly significant that chapter seven, while opening a new phase of the book by its predictive emphasis, is nevertheless still written in Aramaic. This indicates that its message is aimed at the peoples of the world at large. Take note that chapter seven, though again addressing the issue of world empires, focuses on a more distant future than the chapters that preceded it. In particular, we find a major emphasis on the fourth kingdom in the days when God Himself sets up His own everlasting kingdom. Note the chapter's clear division into two large segments: the vision Daniel sees in a dream (vv. 1-14) and its highly promising interpretation (vv. 15-28).

The dream image of chapter two portrayed the unity and continuity of the four world empires. Each is a part of one ongoing program of attempted world dominion. Each is but a new phase of the overall plan of the evil one. Every part of that one image contributes to the whole; without any one, the image would be incomplete. Now those same four empires reappear. But this time we see four separate entities: four beasts. They all emerge from a great sea (v. 3), which the Hebrews would recognize to be the Mediterranean. And it is from tumultuous events transpiring in countries belonging to what we may call the Mediterranean World that these mighty kingdoms arise.

We also find a key passage here (vv. 19-27). This becomes the basis for the Apocalypse of John. A climax is reached with the heavenly court scene (vv. 26-27), resulting from the approaching of the heavenly throne by the risen Christ to receive the everlasting kingdom (vv. 13-14). Interestingly, where Daniel leaves off, giving us intriguing but meager information about the fourth and fifth kingdoms, the book of Revelation picks up and amplifies in great detail. It is not our intent to discuss more fully here the relationship of these two books. For such information, see *The Time Is At Hand* by Jay Adams.

For one special reason, if there were no other, it is of utmost importance to understand this chapter of Daniel. Some of the cults (such as Seventh Day Adventists and Jehovah's Witnesses) and futurist extremists have, in large measure, based and supported their movements on misinterpretations of it.

Once more, using the chart given below, take a good look at the way the book is constructed. Note, in particular, which chapters deal with which kingdoms. Note how the four beasts correspond to the four parts of the metallic image, and how the stone cut out without hands that destroyed the image and filled the entire earth, corresponds to the establishment of God's kingdom with its authority over all the nations. Note also that the heavenly court takes away the dominion of the four kingdoms in the days of the fourth. The fourth one, in particular, is judged at that time, just as the stone, by smashing its feet, topples the entire image at the time of the fourth kingdom. But in both of these special revelations from God, the *fifth* kingdom is the one that is everlasting and irreplaceable.

Overall, we can see that the earlier chapters of Daniel, the accounts narrated in the first half of his book, have to do with events contemporary to the writer. That's why Nebuchadnezzar's obviously prophetic dream vision is included there. But the remaining half of the book of Daniel looks forward, for the most part, to the period following Daniel's lifetime—up to and including the coming of the Messiah.

Prophetic Visions of Daniel

Aramaic Part (22:4-7:28)			**Hebrew Part** (Ch. 2-12)	
Chapter 2		**Chapter 7**	**Chapter 8**	**Chapter 9**
Dream Image		Vision of 4 Beasts	2 Beasts	70 Weeks
Gold Head	**Babylon**	Winged Lion		
Silver Breast	**Medo-Persia**	Lopsided Bear	2 Horned Ram	Jerusalem & Temple
Brass Torso	**Greece**	4-headed Leopard	He-Goat (Large horn to 4; little one grows	
Iron & Tile legs & feet	**Rome**	10-horned Monster & Little Horn (Roman Emperor)		
Stone fells image & fills all earth	**God's Everlasting Kingdom**	4 Beasts judged Rule given to Christ and His people at Ascention		Messiah (End of OT economy)

We now need to consider the four beasts in order. Obviously, they too represent the now familiar successive empires, Babylon, Medo-Persia, Greece, and Rome.

1. *Babylon.* The lion (v. 4), corresponding to the head of gold (chapter 2), was a most appropriate symbol for Babylon. Huge winged lions, sculpted with human heads, have been excavated by archaeologists. A leonine theme ran through Babylonian art. It is found on their cylinder seals, statues, paintings, tiles, and bricks.

We see its wings were torn off, it was lifted from walking on all fours, standing upright like a man. It is said to have been given a human heart. The symbolism shows that the kingdom of the winged lion had been humbled. A seemingly invincible lionhearted kingdom turned out to be only human after all, and its dominion passed away. Specific reference may also be made to the bringing down of proud Nebuchadnezzar and the defeat of Belshazzar.

2. *Medo-Persia*. The bear (v. 5) corresponds to the chest and arms of silver, Medo-Persia. Attention is called to the two sides of the bear, one raised higher than the other. (That section of the dream image included two arms.) Yet here the imagery is even more specific, with the upraised side of the bear representing the Persian part of the kingdom, because under Cyrus it soon gained ascendancy over the Median half of the coalition (cf. 8:3). The three ribs in the bear's mouth most likely represent three other kingdoms devoured by this Medo-Persian empire—Babylon, Egypt, and Lydia (cf. 8:4).

3. *Greece*. The leopard (or panther) is Greece, corresponding to the thighs of brass. This animal stands for Alexander's Hellenistic empire that stretched from the Indus River to the Nile. Its wings signal the great speed with which this young military genius, who died at age 33, established his empire. A pupil of the famous Aristotle, Alexander of Macedonia extended his rule farther than all who had come before him in a span of just twelve years.

The four wings and four heads of this beast also represent the four divisions into which the vast empire was broken at the death of Alexander. The four were headed up by his outstanding generals: Cassander (Greece and Macedonia), Lysimachus (Thrace and Asia Minor), Seleucus (Syria and much of Asia), and Ptolemy (Egypt and Palestine). Daniel has a great deal more to say about these last two dynasties, since their political and military clashes across the years involve God's people in the Holy Land, once the latter became reestablished there.

4. *The Nondescript Beast*. This terrifying creature (vv. 7ff.) is Rome, the iron-and-tile legs and feet of the metallic image seen in Nebuchadnezzar's dream. It remains mysterious and nameless throughout Daniel's book, since in Daniel's time it had not yet become a power and was virtually unknown to the Jews. At the same time, in this chapter it is the main concern over and above the other kingdoms. It is said to be "different" from the others. How?

The answer is in its ferocious appearance and that it had "ten horns." Again, this corresponds to the image—the ten toes of the iron-and-tile feet. Both symbols reveal that the government of the Roman world empire would not be centered in a single authority. As we observe from history, it had no king. It was a republic, in which the senate ruled. Moreover, in time it was divided into ten provinces, each ruled by a puppet "king" (such as Herod, in Palestine; Archelaus, of Matt. 2:22, and "King Agrippa" in Acts 25:13) appointed by the emperor. Revelation 17:12 depicts them ruling *as* "kings for one hour," something less than true sovereigns. It is "the beast" who, in Revelation, chapters 13 and 17, appears to be a composite of all Daniel's beasts.

Careful attention must be given to some parallels. As here in Daniel 7, in Revelation 13 and 17, the beast has ten horns. The horns' role is contemporaneous in both books. We are told they give power to the beast and reign with him for an hour (that is, briefly). But eventually they devour him. That the Roman Empire was destroyed by tribes from her own provinces is a fact of history. The "little horn" (v. 8), who had shrewdness of insight and a "big mouth" (cf. v. 20), and was full of greed and pride, persecuted God's people for three and a half years (historically, from November, 64 AD, to June, 68 AD, at his death) and was finally judged by God (vv. 21-22).

Daniel's little horn is Revelation's eighth head. The change from horn to head allows John to give more information, to help us identify the horn, or head, or beast, as he is variously called. In this way, John can peg him as a certain one of a series of emperors—the last of the Caesar dynasty. He is precisely identified as "666" (Rev. 13:18). This is the very number reached when you add the numerical values of the letters in *neron kaiser* (Nero Caesar).[1]

In both Daniel's prophecy and Revelation, the beast's appearance is followed by the establishment of Christ's kingdom. Therefore, from today's vantage point, these things took place in the past. The setting up of the fifth kingdom resulted from Christ's ascension, as He came with clouds to the throne of God, the Ancient of Days, in heaven—not to

1 For full documentation on this, see *The Time Is At Hand*, p. 92.

earth. This took place after human eyes could no longer see Him (Acts 1:9). It happened on the other side of the cloud that received Him. He was then and there invested as King of kings and Lord of lords, the risen God-man, Who is even now ruling the world. The blood-bought saints of God at the same time constituted the worldwide kingdom or *empire* of God.

This is precisely what Jesus announced to His disciples after His resurrection and shortly before His ascension: "All authority in heaven and on earth has been given to Me. Go, therefore, and make disciples from all nations …" (Matt. 28:18-19). And six days prior to His transfiguration (a foretaste of His ascension glory), He directed to Peter, with the others, the promise, "… on this rock I will build My church, and the gates of Hades will not prevail against it. I will give you the keys of the empire from the heavens, and whatever you bind on earth shall have been bound in the heavens, and whatever you loose on earth shall have been loosed in the heavens" (Matt. 16:18-19).

We therefore live in an age of great promise, of high expectation, and of grave responsibility! Our Lord, the King, has said the gates of Hell itself shall prove powerless to prevent not only the survival or the growth of His empire on earth, "My church," as He named it. In spite of afflictions, persecutions, and seeming setbacks, for which He also has prepared us (Acts 14:22; 2 Tim. 3:12), ours is a very positive, optimistic outlook. We need only think about the blessed assurance John was inspired to give those threatened churches in Asia in addressing the Revelation to them. His praise to "Jesus Christ, the Faithful Witness, the First-born of the dead and the Ruler of the kings of the earth" is as follows:

> *To Him Who loves us and has freed us from our sins by His blood, and made us a kingdom, priests to His God and Father, to Him be glory and might forever and ever. Amen.*
>
> (Revelation 1:5-6)

At the close of this vital chapter, a sober reflection seems in order. You may wonder, "If this grand empire of God was His aim all along, why was He so patient or permissive with the others, those designed and controlled by the fallen angel, Satan? Is not His sovereignty called into question throughout the period dominated by a succession of evil empires?" Hardly. Put more forcefully, as Paul would say it, "Of course not!" (Rom. 3:4, 6, 31; 6:2, 15, and elsewhere).[2]

Let Paul himself speak to the issue. To those in the region of Lycaonia who were about to offer sacrifices to Barnabas (as Zeus!) and to Paul (as Hermes/Mercury), he warned, "We are announcing the good news to you to turn from these empty things to a living God, Who made the sky and the earth and the sea and everything in them." To this he adds, "In past generations He allowed the Gentiles to go their own ways" (Acts 14:15-16). Shortly thereafter, passing through Macedonia and on southward into Greece (not without further opposition and afflictions), Paul arrives at Athens, where he delivers his famous discourse in the council of the Areopagus. Once again the apostle announces,

> *God overlooked*[3] *the times of ignorance, but now He declares that every human being everywhere must repent, because He has set a day in which He is going to judge the world with justice by a Man Whom He has designated to do so. And He has furnished proof of this to everybody by resurrecting Him from the dead.*
>
> (Acts 17:30-31)

---

2 Read for yourself the ninth chapter of Romans and also *The Grand Demonstration: A Biblical Study of the So-called Problem of Evil*, by Jay Adams.

3 The "overlooking" mentioned here does not mean condoning or ignoring sin. It simply refers to the fact that God had not yet brought full punishment upon them.

Chapter 8
The Greek Dominion

What's going on here? Daniel has suddenly switched back to the Hebrew language to tell his story. There must be a reason why he does so—from here to the end of the book. We mentioned this in the Introduction.

A large central portion is written in Aramaic, announcing in the *lingua franca* of many nationalities that God is sovereign over all. The opening chapter and the final ones, beginning here at chapter eight, are written in Daniel's native Hebrew, directed to his own people. They speak of how world affairs will affect them, and how all this is to be resolved by their coming Messiah.

Remember, the overriding theme of this book is not how great a man Daniel was, but that God alone is sovereign over the affairs of men. He puts down one king and raises up another. All that had been going on in the world's history was the story of what God had been doing. And through His prophet Daniel, He was assuring His people that He had control of the future as well.

There are several principles that can be gleaned from what we have already covered in the book of Daniel. They help us view world events from a Christian, biblical worldview. It is vital that we see things from the Bible's perspective, not from that of other worldly philosophies. Many have tried to tell us how to view human history, be it Edward Gibbon (*Decline and Fall of the Roman Empire*), H. G. Wells (*Outline of History*), Arnold Toynbee (*Study of History*), or Will Durant (*Story of Civilization*). Only from the biblical perspective can we see the rest of the story, and the best of the story; only the Bible gives us the facts as God knows and determines them. And where can we better get the biblical view of world history than in this book of Daniel?

We'll suggest five principles for understanding history. You could find these in the Bible yourself, and you may wish to add one or two more. Think how the following are derived and apply:

1. God's *sovereignty* means that nothing takes place outside of His plan. "Things" work out His way, not of themselves. (For some, this may raise an issue. If God is always sovereign, in full charge, why do we speak of these nations as being Satan-dominated? Why is Satan called "the god of this age" [2 Cor. 4:4]?) It must be recognized that when Adam yielded to the will of the Evil One, it was his own assigned dominion on earth that he surrendered, not that of the Creator. Christ came to bring down Satan, reclaiming dominion on earth on behalf of His heirs, the believers.
2. Daniel's book speaks about the coming Greek and Roman empires, how they will serve to bring about *His* purposes.
3. God uses events to *chasten* His people: exile in Babylon was His instrument to drive idolatry from their midst.
4. History is *not cyclical*, nor is it simply the impact of a series of great thinkers and leaders. (Yet even one of our Christmas carols has a pagan Greek line, "And with the ever circling years, comes round the age of gold"!) Rather, we are moving toward the *denouement* (final solution), when all things will be gathered together under Christ.
5. All events and facts are not of equal weight or value. Each must be *interpreted* according to God's revealed purpose and plan for His people. (Ahab is a good example: he has a big place in Bible history, but small in secular records; Omri, his father, has slight mention in the Bible, wider recognition in extrabiblical inscriptions.)

Be assured, what you do today, hearing or reading God's Word to learn His ways and purposes, can be of greater value and influence than a person's going to his or her business office to make decisions involving huge sums of money. It is of first importance to think about and to be about the Father's business, to represent Him at home and in the marketplace. When at last the linear ages do come to an end, in Christ, values will be reckoned correctly, and in many cases, the weights will be completely reversed.

We shall now look at the third of the parallel prophetic images. The first was the four-part giant statue of Nebuchadnezzar's dream; the second was the four beasts Daniel saw emerging from the sea; and this one focuses on just two animals seen in combat. Here, in the second vision he received during Belshazzar's reign (8:1[b]), Daniel was given information about the second and third great imperial kingdoms, especially the third—the Greek dominion.

Why the concentration on the period of Greek expansion? The facts of history are these: Babylon was about to fall to the Medo-Persian power, which would be overtaken by Alexander, the Greek conqueror from Macedonia. Rome would succeed the period of Greek domination, but the details of the Roman Empire period, still far off, would be dealt with in the Revelation of the Risen Lord to John. So it's in preparation for the great persecution which God's people were to suffer after their resettlement in Judea that Daniel's book, from here to the end, is written. That troublesome time is brought on by successors to Alexander—one of them in particular.

Chapter nine will establish a framework, a timeline along which or within which all the series of predictions contained in this remarkable book will be fulfilled. It will center upon the Holy City, Jerusalem, and the redemption to be accomplished there by the Anointed One, Messiah Jesus. Remember that all these latter chapters are written in the Hebrew language and are, therefore, directed to the nation of Israel. They'll sorely need this information as events unravel; so do we, as we study them.

Daniel was at the palace of Shushan (Susa) in Elam, a chief province of Persia, when he received this vision in a dream. This provided a fitting context for what he saw, standing there on the bank of the Ulai River. We read his description:

> *When I raised my eyes I caught sight of a strong ram standing at the riverside. He had a pair of horns, high ones, but one was higher than the other—the higher one rising up afterwards. I saw the ram thrusting westward, and toward the north and toward the south; and no crea-*

> *tures could stand before him. There was none who could deliver from his might, for he did what he pleased and became great.*
>
> (8:3-4)

We are told in the interpretation given to Daniel (v. 20) that this ram, whose two horns are mentioned, represents the kings of Media and Persia. These are apparently Darius the Mede (5:31) and Cyrus the emperor, who "rose higher" in power over the Persian kingdom. The directions of expansion named in the vision are historically precise, as this was an eastern power "butting" its way toward the Mediterranean region. Daniel's vision became even more animated:

> *While I was pondering, behold, a shaggy male goat came from the west over the surface of the whole land, but he wasn't touching the ground. The goat had a conspicuous horn between his eyes.*
>
> (v. 5)

This was the "first king" of the even more expansive Greek empire, none other than mighty Alexander the Great (v. 21). His entrance was from the west, of course, and the rapidity of his military exploits is expressed by the appearance of the goat's charge—he was not even touching the ground. Within twelve years his forces advanced from the Mediterranean coast into India. His fame and fear spread throughout the entire Near East and Mediterranean Basin.

In the next verse we are told that the goat approached the ram with the two horns and ran at him "with furious strength." Further details were given as Daniel continues his report:

> *Then I saw him strike at the ram. He was embittered against him, bashing the ram so as to break his two horns; and the ram did not have strength to stand before him. So he threw him to the ground and trampled him. Nor was there anyone to deliver from his might.*
>
> (v. 7)

The superlatives with which Daniel describes the creatures of his vision sound like unrealistic exaggerations, until the facts about Alexander's campaigns are known. His 35,000 troops destroyed the huge Persian army of over a million men in 331 BC. The Persians had the advantage of fighting on familiar ground and with local supplies available. This mighty warrior "became exceedingly great" indeed. Even the Icelanders and the Japanese have retained legends about Alexander.

Educated under the great philosopher Aristotle and heir at age twenty to the throne of his father, Philip of Macedon, Alexander became the first king of the extensive Hellenistic (Greek) empire. His embittered and crushing attack (v. 7) on the Persians gave Alexander long-awaited revenge for their earlier aggressions, especially for the invasion of Greek soil by Xerxes in 480 BC. (A year later, Esther was queen to this man, the KJV's "Ahasuerus.")

For all this amazing success, Alexander's personal satisfaction and prospect of further exploits were cut short. He died in Babylon at age thirty-three, victim of his own excess with alcoholic drink. Our Lord's death at that age was for our redemption. What a contrast. We are told what happened to the one conspicuous horn centered on the goat's forehead:

> *And the shaggy male goat became exceedingly great; but when he had achieved strength, the large horn was broken off. And in its place four conspicuous ones came up toward the four winds of the heavens. (v. 8)*

The *four* prominent horns on the goat still represent the Greek Empire or Hellenistic Age. History records that at Alexander's death, the territory he controlled was divided among his four major generals (recall the four-headed leopard of chapter seven): Cassander, Lysimachus, Seleucus, and Ptolemy. In other words, we now have four sub-kingdoms within an empire, listed in order of the men just named:

1. Thrace and Macedonia (Western or European): Cassander
2. Asia Minor (Northern): Lysimachus
3. Syria to India (Eastern): Seleucus
4. Egypt (Southern): Ptolemy

Why would God give such a vision to Daniel, two centuries ahead of its realization? Daniel and his Hebrew countrymen were concerned about how to find freedom from exile. Would they ever be resettled in their homeland? Of what personal and practical use to them were these details about still another foreign power? We may find ourselves asking a similar question about many passages of Scripture, especially when the words sound like a riddle.

Have you ever sought directions from a farmer out in the countryside? When you asked, "How do I find such-and-such a place (or person)?" how did he answer? He surely did not come out with a street name, house number, and precise mileage. No. "Go on down the road a piece," he says, "and when ya see a big red barn with an old Mailpouch Tobacco ad on it, you'll turn left right there. Can't miss it. Then a bit farther on—watch them curves, they's like ta throw ya—you'll get ta Sam's turkey farm. Can't miss it. He's got a sign hangin' out by the road, says 'Sam's Turkey Farm.' Place you want is the next farm, right next ta Sam's. Name's on the mailbox, right-hand side. Can't miss it." In other words, you received visual points and objects that would guide you and assure you you were on the right track, till you reached a desired destination. In the same way, God gives some identifying features of future events, so that when they happen, His people will know that this is the very path He has mapped out for them, even though it entails persecution by satanic world kingdoms. They need never think, "The world is out of control." Rather, they can say, "This is exactly what He told us to expect."

So, some two hundred years later, the people of God saw a great conqueror, Alexander, who smashed the Persian Empire, trampling it underfoot, all with amazing swiftness. There's the red barn with the Mail Pouch ad. As events took a turn, Alexander died and was succeeded by four heads of separate states. Sam's Turkey Farm comes into view, so we know we've come the right route. God gave (gives) His people assurance that everything is happening according to plan, according to His program—the way it was *meant* to happen. There would be rough times ahead for them, but they needed to know things were *not* out of control.

Not all the details are spelled out in the prophetic vision, of course. There was a struggle of some twenty years before the four military leaders could lay claim to precise borders. It is said that Alexander named no successor. His vague pronouncement, "For the one who deserves it," probably implied he judged none to be his match.

Verses 9 through 18 and 23 through 27 of chapter eight focus more closely on a particular successor to one of those four leaders who divided up Alexander's realm. So important is this particular king that we shall meet him again in the final chapters of Daniel's book. He is here introduced as a "Little Horn" that grows way out of proportion.

We learn more about what Daniel saw in verses 9-19 and 23-27 of chapter eight:

> *Then from one of them there came up a single small horn, but it became exceedingly large—toward the south and toward the east and toward the splendid [land].* (v. 9)

This, we must observe, is a different "Little Horn" from that described in chapter seven (vv. 8 and 20ff.). That one was associated with the fourth beast from the sea, the Roman Empire. Throughout chapter eight, we are dealing with the second and third empires, and this horn relates to one of the four successors of Alexander, in the third, or Greek, kingdom period. (Why horns? Not only do they fit the beast imagery, but they also are symbols of power.) The "splendid land" refers, of course, to what we know as the Holy Land. "Holy Land" occurs only once in the KJV Bible (Zech. 2:12), though the NIV so translates Psalm 78:54 as well. The nature and behavior of this horn (ruler) is revealed:

> *So it grew up to the heavenly host and threw to the earth some of the stars of the hosts, and trampled on them. And he made himself great as the Prince of the host, and from Him he removed the continual sacrifice, and the place of His sanctuary was cast out. Moreover, a rebellious host was placed over the continual sacrifice, and truth was cast to the ground; so it functioned and prospered.*
> (vv. 10-12)

This cannot be a description of Alexander. He was not of this sort. Tradition has it that as Alexander marched toward Jerusalem after seizing the Philistine ("Palestinian") coast, he was met by the High Priest and his company. When the Jews showed him that his career was predicted in the prophecies of sacred Scriptures, he counted himself honored and blessed; so he chose to do nothing blasphemous against the Holy City of God.

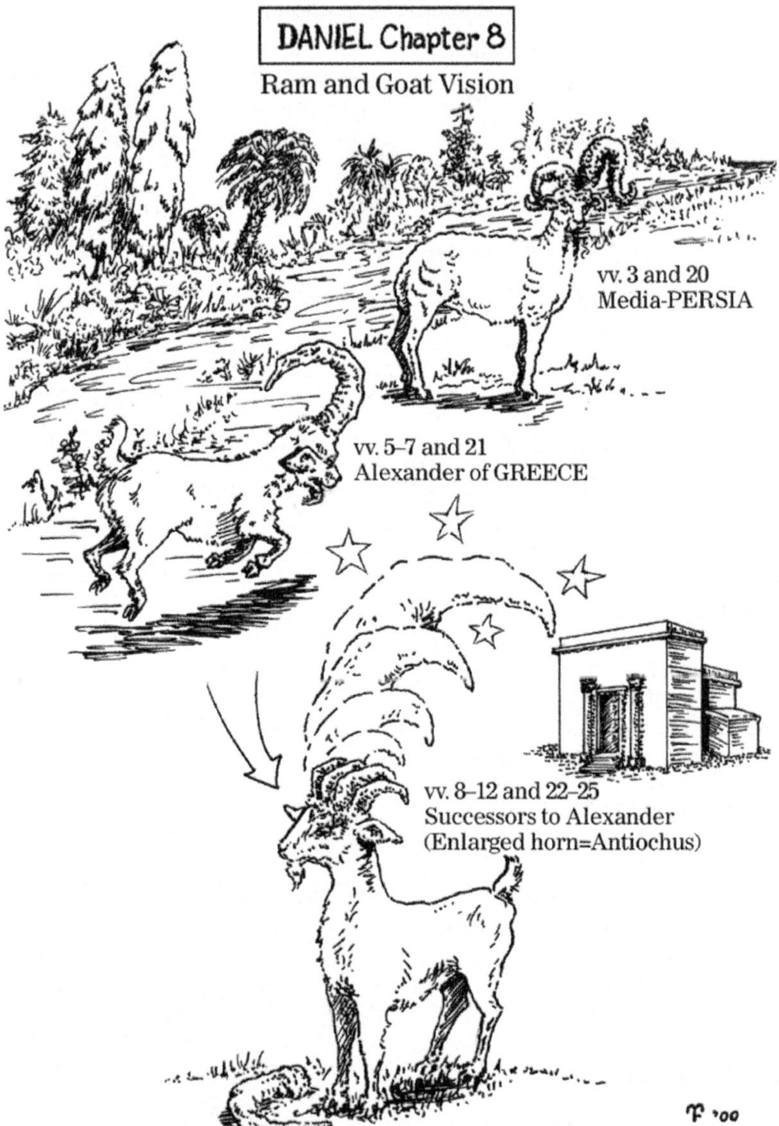

The overgrown, overbearing, and destructive little horn represents, rather, the eighth ruler in the Seleucid or Syrian segment of the Greek Empire. This ruler, Antiochus Epiphanes ("Glorious One"), was called Antiochus Epimenes ("Madman") behind his back. He invaded Judea in the process of contending with the ruler of the South (Egypt). He cast truth to the ground by killing key leaders of God's people and causing temple sacrifices to cease as of June 5th, 167 BC. Bent on turning Palestine into a Greek community, Antiochus set up a gymnasium near the temple, where the abomination of having naked athletes perform was bad enough; but he pushed on to the purposeful desecration of the temple by sacrificing a pig on the altar, then sprinkling pork broth all around the sacred precincts. When such horrible things suddenly came upon God's people, including His sacred temple, the people needed to be ready to handle them. That's where the big red barn and Sam's Turkey Farm come in. This is just what God foretold, in the imagery of vision. Verse 13 answers the natural question, "How long? Will this go on forever?!"

> *Then I heard one holy one speaking, and another holy one said to that one who spoke, How long is the vision about the continual sacrifice and the destructive rebellion which allows both the holy place and the host to be trampled?*

God certainly isn't going to dwell in such a desecrated sanctuary. The answer comes immediately, in verse 14:

> *And he said to me, Until two thousand and three hundred evening-mornings; then the holy place will be reconsecrated [literally: justified].*

From the beginning of Antiochus' attack on the religion of the covenant people to the cleansing of the temple, December 25, 164 BC, we have the 2,300 days (exactly six years, three months, and twenty days). Antiochus was driven out of the Holy Land, he died, and God's place was once again made holy. The 1,290 days of chapter 12, verse 11, correspond to the three-and-a-half years of the desecration of the temple itself.

The evil Antiochus had tried to wipe out Judaism altogether. He not only interfered with temple worship but also forbade possession of the Scriptures, burning all he could find; he forbade circumcision of Jewish sons, and he stripped the temple of its sacred vessels. Jupiter's statue was erected in the holy of holies. He killed and enslaved tens of thousands of Jews (the stars he cast down were godly leaders), but he himself was cut off. God was and is still on His throne.

Poor Daniel was still struggling to understand. We read:

> *And when I, Daniel, had seen the vision and was seeking understanding, behold, the appearance of a strong man stood in front of me. Then I heard a man's voice at the Ulai, which called out and said, "Gabriel, enable this one to understand what appeared." So he came near where I was standing, and when he approached, I was afraid and I fell on my face. But he said to me, "Understand, son of man, that the vision is for the time of the end."*
>
> (vv. 15-17)

These last words are crucial. We know from history (books of Maccabees, Josephus, etc.) the time when these predicted conditions and events were precisely fulfilled, near the close of the Old Testament age. So for Daniel and his readers, "the time of the end" has to mean the close of the Jewish, Mosaic, Old Covenant period of history. The writer of Hebrews in the New Testament declares this as well—very dramatically so at 12:25-29, speaking with reference to Jesus, the Mediator of a newly established covenant:

> *See to it that you do not refuse to hear the One Who speaks. If they didn't escape when they refused to listen to the one who warned them on earth, how much less will we if we turn away from the One Who warns us from the heavens? At one time, His voice shook the earth, but now He has promised, "Once more I will shake not only the earth, but heaven too!" Now, "once more" indicates the removal of what is shaken (created things, that is), so that what can't be shaken may remain. Therefore, let us be thankful that we have received an unshakable em-*

> *pire, and let us serve God in a manner that pleases Him with reverence and awe. For our God is a consuming fire!*

Daniel describes the shock to his physical being:

> *While he was speaking with me I had fallen into a deep sleep with my face to the ground, so he touched me and stood me upright.*
> (v. 18)

We've already learned what Daniel was told in the succeeding verses, that the ram was Medo-Persia, and the goat was Alexander's vast domain—divided into four parts. We pick up at verse 23:

> *And in the latter part of their kingdom, when the transgressors are at their worst, a king of severe countenance will stand forth, one who understands intrigue. Now his power will be mighty, but not by his own strength; he will be amazingly destructive, for he will succeed in what he does: he will destroy mighty men, even the holy people.*
> (vv. 23-24)

Even such an evil worker has no power but by God's sovereign permission. We've reviewed all that was done by Antiochus Epiphanes to erase true religion from earth, both by deadly persecution and by corrupt substitutions of false religion and culture. Such attacks have continued throughout church history and into our own day, communism and Islam being the most recent perpetrators. His end is again declared at the conclusion of verse 25:

> *And because of his skill he will cause deceit to prosper by his hand, and by magnifying his ego he will destroy many who are unsuspecting. He'll even stand against the Prince of princes; but without [visible] hand he shall be broken.*

His taking a bold stand against God Himself (though some take Prince to mean Gabriel) proved to be the wicked ruler's undoing. God brings him down, as we shall see later in the book. An important order is given to Daniel at verse 26, a key to interpretation:

> *Now the revelation of the evening and the morning which was spoken is truth: you must conceal the vision, for it is for yet many days.*

It was, for Daniel and his compatriots, a long way into the future when these predicted events would transpire; nearly four centuries passed before Antiochus came to power. So Daniel was told to seal up his scroll, that it might serve a far future generation. This command is repeated in the final chapter, at 12:9:

> *Then he said, Go, Daniel, for the words are closed and sealed until the time of the end.*

The contrast could not be sharper than that which we find in the closing chapter of the Revelation to John:

> *And he said to me, "Don't seal the words of the prophecy of this scroll, since the time is at hand."*
>
> (Rev. 22:10)

This is what brings these two fascinating prophetic books into juxtaposition historically. Daniel speaks of the events at the close of one era and Revelation to those at the opening of the next. The high point of Daniel is the heavenly throne scene of chapter seven, while Revelation opens with and features throughout that same glorious setting.

Chapter eight closes with Daniel's testimony to how stressful it had been to be given such frightful and bewildering glimpses into the future. Great kingdoms arose, flourished, then crashed in quick succession before him. Yet he was to live to see only the early stages thereof. The chapter ends on this note, at verse 27:

> *Then I, Daniel, fell sick for days, but I rose up and performed the king's business. I remained dumbstruck concerning the vision, for it was beyond comprehension.*

Centuries later, as we shall see, there would be those righteous and enlightened ones who would read Daniel's words, would realize exactly what was going on, and would stand for the truth and resist evil opposition. They would be the victors, and they would form the link between the early saints of Israel and those who would, within the next two centuries, welcome Israel's long-awaited Messiah.

Chapter 9
Countdown Toward the End

DANIEL knew his Bible, and he knew the Bible had answers to the plight of his exiled people. Though he himself had achieved high reputation and status over the years, and only recently had survived a major change of a government's administration, he was more concerned about his own nation. Above all, he held in highest priority the honor of his God. For this reason, he had searched the Scriptures for answers.

Thus, in the very first year of Darius the Mede, governor of Babylon, Daniel seized upon the promise in Jeremiah's prophecy that precisely 70 years had been set as the term of Jerusalem's punitive desolation. The end of that period was now at hand. So Daniel looked to his God with earnest prayer. Use of a concordance makes it easy for us to locate what Daniel had searched out:

> *All this land will become a waste and a ruin ... and they will serve the king of Babylon seventy years. But when seventy years have fully come about, says Jehovah, I will call to account for their wrongs the king of Babylon and the people, even the land of the Chaldeans, and render it an everlasting desolation.*
>
> (Jer. 25:11-12)

The Hebrews were taken away as captives because they had broken the terms of their covenant with Jehovah their God. The hearts of the people were estranged from God through the worship of false gods. Another major sign of apostasy was their long-standing failure to observe the covenant sign of the sabbaths—weekly, and in the cycle of years. The latter disobedience is cited as the clear explanation for Judah's destruction at the hands of King Nebuchadnezzar. We find this in 2 Chronicles 36:20-21:

> *And he carried captive to Babylon those whom the sword left, where they became servants to him and to his descendants till the rule of the Persian kingdom, to fulfill Jehovah's word by the mouth of Jeremiah: Until the land enjoys her sabbaths; all the days of the desolation she has rested to fulfill seventy years.*

So, if we take this to mean that Israel had neglected observance of the sabbatical year requirements 70 times, that would extend over a period of 490 years—back to the reign of King Saul. That is quite likely. We are told in 2 Chronicles 35:18 that not since the days of the prophet Samuel had Israel kept such a Passover as did King Josiah—as part of his reformation. The terms of the Mosaic Law had been grossly ignored.

The time of reckoning came, but the nation had now paid her debt (Is. 40:2), so Daniel was anxious for the terms of pardon to be announced. Another 490-year period, the famous "Seventy Weeks," is designated at the end of this ninth chapter of Daniel. God's mercy, in the form of restoration to the Promised Land, was about to be displayed. Daniel here uttered one of the most remarkable prayers in all of Holy Scripture. In this moving prayer, we see both the heart and wisdom of a great man of God.

Why, though, did Daniel plead with God with fasting, and covered with sackcloth and ashes? He knew what Jehovah, his covenant-keeping God, had promised in His Word. A sure prophecy was about to be fulfilled. So why pray? Why not just sit and patiently wait? We face this seeming dilemma constantly ourselves, especially if we believe in God's sovereign decree and control of all that occurs. The answer is obvious. God commands us to pray. He encourages us to pray in faith, believing He knows and does what is best for us. But why does He do that, if He's already determined what He is going to do?

It is clear throughout Scripture and from personal observation that God chooses to work through means. Call it "natural means" or "providence." Only in the case of demonstrative miracles or "signs" does God seemingly bypass the use of some procedure for the accomplishment of His purposes. And even when supernatural intervention occurs, prayer may be involved, as it was in the case of the fiery response to Elijah's prayer on Mount Carmel. Daniel knew this. So he did not hesitate to call on his God to work in response to his prayer. To His own honor and glory, God is pleased to have us come to Him in humble dependence for what we desire—even when it is in direct fulfillment of what He has promised. Our Heavenly Father delights to see us helped and blessed by His answers to our prayers. Furthermore, we are to act responsibly toward the obtaining of what we ask of Him. "Give us this day our daily bread," we beg, knowing that we must work to earn our living (cf. 2 Thess. 3:10). By God's grace we receive the strength and means to do so. All we are and have comes from Him.

So Daniel prayed, making confession for himself and his people:

> *Ah, my Lord, the great and awesome God, Who keeps covenant love for those who love Him and who observe His commands. We have sinned and committed wrongs; we have rebelled; we have been lawless and disobedient, turning away from Your commands and Your judgments. Nor have we heeded Your servants the prophets, who have spoken in Your name to our kings, our princes, and our fathers—to all the people of the land.*
>
> (vv. 4-6)

One godly man prayed on behalf of an entire nation of people. "We ... we ... we ... our ... our ... our ...," he said. This is a great example and encouragement for us, the Christian minority in our increasingly corrupted nation and in a world in need of Christ. Each of us, alone or in small gatherings, can pray expectantly for God to make changes in society. He listens. It is not ours to complain about conditions and to worry about the future for our offspring. That's thinking on the horizontal plane. Believers have vertical access to an all-wise and almighty God, Who can change men's hearts and ways. Most, as were the majority of those Jews in Babylon, are so much "part of the scene" that they seek no change. So it is up to the few who are discerning and are concerned about what *is,* to pray earnestly for what *ought* to be. Of such a mind and spirit was Daniel.

Even as he prayed, many of Daniel's countrymen were heedless of God's commandments and admonitions that had been given to them by

God-inspired prophets down through the centuries of Hebrew history. Lawless, rebellious, and disobedient sinners, Daniel called them. So careless and insensitive were they that God's lone representative had to intercede *for* them, though they would not even be in sympathy with what he prayed. The same problem exists in our day, throughout society, and even in the churches. People don't know or care what the Bible has to say. Many will laugh at it, considering it old-fashioned and irrelevant. Judgment is due for such a defiant spirit. The church of today is responsible to proclaim the Word prophetically, and to pray. "Dare to be a Daniel," in other words.

Notice how the nation's leaders were primarily responsible: "Nor have we heeded Your servants the prophets, who have spoken in Your name to our kings, our princes, and our fathers" (v. 6). This is followed by "—even to all the people of the land," which is represented today by all the members of Christ's church. The Apostle Peter reminds us, "it is time for judgment to begin with God's household" (1 Peter 4:17). Daniel saw a general breakdown of covenant loyalty to Israel's God, from the top on down. What do you see—starting with yourself, your family, and on up?

Beginning at verse 7, Daniel went on to confess the shamefacedness of his people—in stark contrast to the uprightness of their God, coupled with His great mercy and forgiveness:

> *To You, Lord, belongs righteousness; to us shame of face, as at this day, to every Judaean, even to the inhabitants of Jerusalem and to all of Israel—those who are near and those far away in all the lands to which You have expelled them because of the unfaithfulness they have shown toward You. Yes, Lord, to us belongs shame of face—to our kings, to our princes, and to our fathers, who have sinned against You. With the Lord our God is mercy and pardon, though we have disobeyed Him. Nor have we harkened to the voice of Jehovah our God, to walk according to His laws, which He has placed before us by means of His servants the prophets. For all Israel has transgressed Your law and turned aside, so as not to give heed to your voice. Therefore, the curse is poured out on us, even the sworn oath which is written in the Law of Moses, the servant of God, because we have sinned against Him.*

Notice that the leaders of the land (and of the church) would be held responsible in a special sense for national waywardness; but so shall *all* the people of the land, as well. Daniel prayed for every last one, beginning at the top and including himself. These folks were all well aware that very early in their history as a nation, just as they had entered the Promised Land, in fact, they were given clear and fair warning. Upon renewal of the Sinai covenant at Mounts Gerizim and Ebal (Deut. 11:29-32; Joshua 8:32-35), the consequences of failure to obey God's laws were rehearsed by the second generation and for succeeding generations.

The blessings for covenant obedience would include a peaceful and prosperous life in the land. The curses included pestilence, famine, and invasion, leading to horrible cannibalism, death by the sword, and captivity (exile). The people of Israel had all this read out to them. They had opportunity to choose. They had chosen the wrong way. So their city was devastated, their temple destroyed, their people dragged away to far-off places—families scattered abroad—as the curses had forewarned. Daniel put it this way in his prayer:

> *And He has executed His words which He spoke against us and against our judges who ruled us, to bring upon us a great calamity, such as has not been done under the entire heaven, even that which has been done to Jerusalem. All this wretched calamity has come upon us according to what was written in the Law of Moses; yet we have not sought to placate Jehovah our God, that we might turn from our wrongs and learn to prosper through Your truth. Jehovah was ready with the destruction, to bring it upon us, because Jehovah our God is righteous in every act He performs; but we have not heeded His voice.*
>
> (vv. 12-14)

Now all this judgment had fallen on them. Still they were unrepentant. They had failed to be moved by the truth of God's almighty Word. So Daniel, agonized by the bitter truth, prayed on their behalf. He freely confessed, "Jehovah our God is righteous in every act He performs; but we have not heeded His voice." We need to pray like that—first for our own selves, then for our church, and then for our nation.

"How can I pray for a nation so set in ungodly ways and so unrepentant?" you say. Dare to be a Daniel. That's exactly what he was doing. He was praying for an unrepentant people, expecting God to bless them in spite of themselves. He yearned for God first to bring them to repentance, then to bless them. Daniel was a lone man praying earnestly for his people: shake them, wake them, till they see their sin and guilt, and repent. That was the intent of their suffering exile. In time, God did answer Daniel's prayer, as his prophecy predicts and as history later records.

Daniel's prayer intensified, as he uttered strong reasons for his plea—valid theological reasons, we may say.

> *So now, O Lord our God, Who has brought Your people out of Egypt with a mighty hand and made a name for Yourself, as it is this day, we have sinned; we have acted irresponsibly. O Lord, in keeping with all Your righteousnesses, please let Your anger and Your fury turn from Your City Jerusalem, Your own Holy Mountain, for by reason of our sins and by reason of the wrongs of our fathers, Jerusalem and Your people have become an object of scorn to all who are around us.*
>
> *Listen, now, our God, to the prayer of Your servant and to his supplications, and make Your face shine upon Your desolate Sanctuary, for Your own sake.*
>
> (vv. 15-17)

Here is the basis upon which his plea rests. Jehovah God made a mighty name, a grand reputation for Himself by defeating the gods and Pharaoh of Egypt. Now that reputation was being questioned, that name slandered by heathen nations which once had feared the strength and glory that was Israel. So Daniel prayed, without uplifting himself or the past greatness of his nation. He argued not that they had suffered enough, but he reminded God that it was His good name that was at stake—"for Your own sake."

Ungodly people were now wagging their heads and clucking their tongues, uttering shameful proverbs against the desolate land and seemingly abandoned people of God. The Temple of God was in ruins, strewn across a barren waste. The God once worshipped there was now being made fun of. What's more—Jehovah had made a promise, through Jeremiah: captivity would end after 70 years were up. This was what moved Daniel to pray this prayer at the outset. What, then, if He failed to keep that promise?

There was another reason for Daniel's confidence. He prayed not only for the name and honor of God, but also because he knew his was a God of great mercy, and a God of love. Daniel knew, also from the record in the Holy Scriptures, that Jehovah, the covenant-keeping God, had often poured out His mercy upon just such a sinful bunch as these confused Judaeans. Daniel knew the mercy of his God was so great that He could have answered that this seemingly futile prayer of his for so sinful, neglectful, and unrepentant a body of people.

With this in mind, Daniel pleaded,

> *Incline Your ear, O my God, and hear; open Your eyes and see our desolations, even the City which has Your name. For it is not for our righteousnesses that we offer our supplications before You, but because of Your great compassion"* (v. 18).

Do we, today, realize that God's mercy is great enough to turn this nation of ours back to Him? Not our praying itself, but the mercy of God is great enough to answer our prayer that He would do something for this country. God's mercy is greater than all the sin of all time, were it heaped in one pile. It is beyond description. His covenant faithfulness includes merciful forgiveness as well as righteous judgment. All of God's attributes measure up to absolute and holy perfection. Daniel was confident of this as he added,

> *Hear, O Lord; pardon, O Lord; O Lord, hearken and act without delay—for Your own sake, O my God; for Your City and Your people bear Your name"* (v. 19).

It no doubt surprises those who never bothered to take note, but Daniel's prayer takes up two-thirds of chapter nine. Most folks overlook the significance of this very special prayer in their haste to move along to the intriguing part at the end of the chapter. That's the part about the

"Seventy weeks." Yet it is this prayer's content which prepares the way for and literally invites God's response—a reply which provides one of the most precise and important prophecies about the work of the Messiah to be found anywhere in the Old Testament.

Suddenly, Daniel, the prayer warrior, was interrupted. We'll never know whether he had more he wanted to say, but God had now heard enough. Let Daniel tell us what happened.

> *And while I was still speaking, praying and confessing my sin and the sin of my people Israel, offering supplications before Jehovah my God concerning the Holy Mountain of my God, even as I was still speaking in prayer, in a state of exhaustion, just then the man Gabriel, whom I had seen at the first in a vision, touched me at the time of the evening offering. He informed me, speaking with me and saying, Daniel, I have come forth to enable you to understand.*
>
> (vv. 20-22)

Daniel had poured himself out in prayer to the point of exhaustion, as expressed in our translation of verse twenty-one. Similar stress is reported by Daniel in connection with some of his other encounters with God, in connection with visions sent by the Almighty. These can be found, for example, in 7:15, 28; 8:27; and 10:8-11, 15-17. Would that we today were more deeply moved by what we receive from God's hand as we read His Holy Word.

Gabriel had come, of course, to aid Daniel—to enable him to understand the manner in which Jehovah would indeed keep His promise. This is a good thing for us as well. We'd never be able to understand either, without his implied explanations as he runs through an outline of the timetable involved in God's answers to the "How?" and "How long?" of Daniel's prayer. We also have the advantages of looking back to the actual fulfillment of prophecy and aid from other passages of Scripture. Daniel was assured right away that his prayer was heard. The angel Gabriel told him, "At the outset of your supplications an order was issued, and I have come to tell you that you are favored. So discern the matter, and come to an understanding of the vision." (v. 23)

The moment he began (and even before that, the prayer itself being by God's design), an answer was determined, given by God. The faithful prayer of this one man, this single individual, is answered with remarkable fullness and effectiveness. For the answer would cover not only Daniel's desire and the needs of his own generation and of many to follow, but also would include the salvation you and I enjoy in Christ our Redeemer.

We learn that Daniel was "favored," beloved, highly esteemed (v. 23). It is worthy of note that Daniel is one of very few examples (such as Enoch and Christ Jesus Himself) about whom Scripture reports nothing negative. Other great Bible heroes, like Abraham, Joseph, David, and Paul, are portrayed for us with all their warts. Not that Daniel was without sin (we've heard his confession), yet he was an instrument ready for God's use. He was the one man in that troubled time whose spiritual life was specially prepared with such a receptive attitude, that he might convey God's important message to his people.

Gabriel had come to provide Daniel a grand anticipation. He told God's man for the hour,

> *Seventy heptads are determined with respect to your people and regarding your Holy City: to conclude transgression and to bring an end to sin, to make atonement for wrong and to bring in everlasting righteousness, to seal up vision and prophecy, and to anoint a Most Holy [One].*[4]
>
> (v. 24)

"Seventy sevens," literally, or "heptads"—seventy periods of seven. This answers "when?" with far greater content than Daniel had in mind. He asked about the restoration of the "earthly tabernacle," the demolished temple of Solomon. God answers Daniel's specific question, but adds far more. The answer takes us on past that temporary restoration to full salvation in Christ and to the final end of the temple, as rebuilt by King Herod. Here and in the latter chapters of Daniel's prophecy, God explains the "Time of the End."

---

4 Compare 1 Chron. 23:13 (NASB), where Aaron is sanctified as "most holy." Hebrew form here in Daniel, as well, differs from "the Holy of Holies" as a place.

The time period involved is expressed in "sevens," seen by nearly all expositors to represent years—counted by clusters of seven. So, 70 times 7 gives us 490 years for the total period. The Judaeans had remained under the judgment of God for 70 years; now Jehovah God's gracious gift of restoration to their homeland, His gift to them in the first place, was assured to them for 7 times that long. Above all, that 490-year period takes them right up to the coming of the "Most Holy," the Messiah Jesus, Who would atone for their sins and for ours.

God's blessings, in Old Testament times as in the New, always outdo His judgment. The principle is asserted in Romans 5:20, where we find, "But where sin abounded, grace far more abounded." So even though they did not deserve it, God would return His covenant people to their land. Six essential things were going to happen with respect to Christ's work of redemption by the time the 70 heptads were fulfilled. God would then:

1. conclude transgression
2. bring an end to sin
3. make atonement for wrong
4. bring in everlasting righteousness
5. seal up vision and prophecy
6. anoint a Most Holy (One)

It is interesting to note that the first three negatives are to be eliminated by the performance of the latter three positives. "Accentuate the positive; eliminate the negative," we used to sing in a popular song. Only our God can meet that demand to the point of perfection.

It is essential for the reader to grasp the practical and personal importance of this passage, and not just to focus on the exciting details of the "Seventy Weeks." Here, most clearly in Daniel's book, the gospel (*good news*) of Jesus Christ is presented. What Daniel anticipates is shown in the New Testament to be fully accomplished by the death of Jesus Christ on the cross.

In the Apocalypse of John, the companion to Daniel's prophetic book, we hear the four "living creatures" of chapters four and five singing a new song to the Lion of the Tribe of Judah:

> *You are worthy … because You were slain, and by Your blood You bought for God persons from every tribe and tongue and people and*

nation, and have made them a kingdom and priests to serve our God, and they reign upon the earth.

(Rev. 5:9-10)

If, as you are reading this, you realize you've not experienced the forgiveness of sins purchased by Christ's atoning death, no part of this book, or Daniel's book itself, is more important for you than this informative description of what Christ was coming to do. If you have not yet trusted Him as Savior, there is no better time to do so than now. The rest of Daniel's message, throughout his book, will be of little profit unless you get right with God through genuine repentance and faith. Daniel's prayer, as explained on the above pages, is a perfect example for you as to how this is done.

Now, opinions may differ on the meaning of certain parts of this "end time" prophecy in Daniel, and in some cases, the very translation of it. But how much clearer could it be that these six benefits are the very things achieved or experienced by our Lord Jesus Christ? Even if the "Most Holy" were taken to be a "place," the fulfillment in His Body, the church, would be by His redemptive work. Yet we shall see that His own anointing, taken to be His baptism by the Levitical priest, John, better fits the total structure of this timeline-oriented prediction.

Gabriel went on to detail the breakdown of time segments within the 70 heptads. He said,

Now know and be enlightened: From the issuing of the order to restore and to rebuild Jerusalem until Messiah the Prince, seven heptads and sixty-two heptads—for again avenues will be constructed, with a moat, yet in times of distress;

(v. 25)

Remember, we are dealing with a total of 490 years ("seventy heptads"), now broken into three parts: 7 heptads (49 years), plus 62 heptads (434 years), leaving one heptad (7 years). We need to find out what happens at each of these three specified periods.

We've been told, at verse 24, that the total period of 490 years had been set by God with respect to Daniel's people and the Holy City in answer to his inquiry about how God planned to bring about the promised restoration. The reply gave Daniel more than he asked for. There was good news—a Redeemer would come; and there was bad—Jerusalem would again be destroyed.

We are told, then, that from a fixed date ("from the issuing of the order to restore and to build Jerusalem—avenues . . . with a moat") there would be 49 years, plus 434 years (483 in all), until the anointing of Messiah[5] the Prince. This should make it possible to determine rather precisely when the Messiah was to begin His redemptive ministry. The problem is, we need to have a starting point from which to count, the *terminus a quo*, as it's technically called.

Many have tried to figure it all out, sometimes with conflicting results. (Others have dodged the problem of arithmetic calculation altogether, suggesting the "weeks" are only figurative, covering the entire sweep of history from Daniel to the end of time.) There must be a more specific reason for such a precise set of numbers. Look what we find, then, using the Scriptures.

At first, the most obvious possibility for the starting point seems to be the initial decree of Cyrus, cited in 2 Chronicles 36:22-23 and Ezra 1:1-4. This decree, issued in the first year of his reign over fallen Babylon, is dated to 538 BC. Subtracting our 483 years from that brings us to 55 BC—far too early for Christ's birth, let alone the start of His public ministry. Besides, Cyrus' decree speaks about the temple, not the finished and fortified city. Furthermore, starting from that decree, the first period of 49 years would take us to 489 BC, too late a date for the construction of the Second Temple, which took place in 536–515 BC.

Due to the "times of distress" forewarned with respect to the restoration of the Holy City, at least three other decrees were issued by Persian rulers. That of Darius, at about 519 BC (Ezra 6:1-12), was only a repetition, by way of confirmation, of Cyrus' original order. Similarly, the decree issued for Nehemiah's benefit by Artaxerxes I (Neh. 2:7-8) in the twentieth year of his reign was only a reaffirmation of his earlier one

5 "Meshiach" means "Anointed One" in Hebrew, and translates to "Christos" (Christ) in Greek.

to Ezra (Ezra 7:11-26) in his seventh year, 457 BC. Some commentators have argued for that later decree of Artaxerxes, using 360-day "prophetic years" for their calculations. The exilic Jews used the Babylonian calendar of 364+ days to the year, making that approach extremely doubtful.

Figure, then, from the first, or 457 BC, decree of Artaxerxes as the starting point. This made it possible for Ezra to defend the city against his contentious neighbors and thus led to the rebuilding of Jerusalem prophesied in verse 25. The 49-year period (first seven heptads) brings us to 408 BC. By then, the avenues and the moat (which assumes walls as well) were completed. The books of Ezra and Nehemiah chronicle the dramatic events of that period—the courageous labors of the returnees, along with their need for spiritual and behavioral reformation.

The longest period of "weeks," the 62 heptads (434 years), during which other momentous events predicted in Daniel transpired, carries us into the period of the Roman Empire. At this point we find ourselves standing on New Testament soil, about to witness a stranger from Galilee at the banks of the Jordan River seeking baptism at the hands of his extraordinary cousin, John. For when we add the 434 to our last reference point, 408 BC, Gabriel has led us, right along with Daniel, to the year 26 AD.

Jesus began His public ministry, you will remember, when He was "about thirty years old" (Luke 3:23). Since He was born around 5 BC (King Herod died in 4 BC) according to the calendar to which our historical dating is erroneously pegged, the timeline announced to Daniel works out with amazing (not surprising) precision. We take the baptism of Jesus, performed by one in the Aaronic priestly line and confirmed by the visible manifestation of the presence of God the Holy Spirit and the voice of God the Father, to be the anointing of this Most Holy One for His prophetic and priestly ministry. Later, speaking of our Lord's bodily resurrection, Peter cried out to the Pentecost crowd, "let the whole house of Israel know for certain that God has made this Jesus Whom you crucified both Lord (that is, King) and Christ" (Acts 2:36). To our Lord Christ belong royal majesty, prophetic authority, and priestly power—by right of His sovereign Person and in the perfect performance of His redemptive work.

We understand this better, after the fact, than Daniel could have in his day, but it was all there in this engrossing prophecy of the "weeks." Still, that most crucial heptad, the seventieth one, remains to entice. Several formulas have been employed in the attempt to explain this one. Some stretch it till it reaches to 70 AD, when the temple was razed by the Romans; and others stretch it so far as to cover the entire church age! Many let it snap completely free, to make its appearance at the end of this age, as a "Great Tribulation" period of seven years duration. This is a huge "gap theory," if you will. Look closely. There is nothing present at all in Gabriel's wording of this outline of the "Seventy Heptads" to suggest or allow for such a break. What we are told is this:

> *And after the sixty-two heptads, Messiah will be cut off, having nothing,*[6] *and the people of the prince who comes will destroy the city and the sanctuary, such that its end is [as] by the flood, for up to the end war is decreed—utter destruction.*
> *Thus He will confirm a covenant with the many for one heptad; yet, in the middle of the heptad, He shall cause sacrifice and offering to cease. And upon a wing shall be a destructive abomination, even to its end. Then what is decreed will be poured out on the destroyer.*
> (vv. 26-27)

"Seventy heptads are determined," said Gabriel at the outset (v. 24), and all six factors of Christ's atoning work were to be accomplished within that time frame. The Anointed One, "Messiah," would be "God's Lamb, Who will take away the world's sins," as John the Baptizer announced (John 1:29). In the Epistle to the Hebrews we are told, "By a single offering He has perfected for all time those who are being set apart," and so "… there is no longer any offering for sins" (Heb. 10:14, 18).

God's messenger then gave a more detailed breakdown of events in Daniel 9:25-26, as we have seen. (Neither Gabriel nor Daniel broke the pronouncement into numbered verses, of course. We sometimes miss

6 This translation is preferred as being in closer harmony with the expanded treatment of this theme in Isaiah 53.

the continuity of a portion of Scripture when we follow a segmented verse-by-verse attempt at interpretation.) Our "verse 26" begins, "And after the sixty-two heptads Messiah will be cut off," and continues with an announcement about Jerusalem's destruction by the armies of Rome ("the people of the prince who comes"). The cutting off or execution of Messiah points us to His cross, on which He gave Himself as the atoning sacrifice for sinners. As we saw in Hebrews, this act put an end to the need for further sacrifices on the temple altar. This is doubtless why, in the same breath, the destruction of the temple is mentioned.

The final verse (v. 27) of this chapter sums up the essentials of Gabriel's presentation of God's plan for His City and people. What is missed by many commentators, and hence by many preachers and teachers, is the continuity of personal subject, from verse 26 into 27. The three grammatical subjects in verse 26 are Messiah, people, and (its) end. Which would you choose as the subject of verse 27—which says, "Thus he (capitalize 'He' if you chose 'Messiah,' as we do) will confirm a covenant with the many for one heptad"—the final one? Messiah is, after all, the most significant and preeminent Person in the whole of this revelation to Daniel.

Who are "the many" with whom He confirms His covenant? Jesus spoke the following words at His last supper with His disciples:

> *"This is My blood of the [new] covenant that is poured out for many."*
> (Mark 14:24)

It takes no stretch of the imagination to say that our Lord had this Daniel passage in mind when He so spoke. The last heptad, beginning with His anointing by baptism for His earthly ministry, is cut short ("in the middle") by His untimely death, humanly speaking, on Calvary's cross. And by that sacrificial death ("once, and once only" Heb. 10:10), Gabriel tells Daniel, "He shall cause sacrifice and offering to cease" (Dan. 9:27). This ties in with the six accomplishments of verse 24.

Back, now, to our dates. We had arrived at 26 AD, approximately, for the start of Jesus' public ministry; and when we add on the three and a half years (half the heptad), we come to an acceptable dating of the crucifixion of our Lord. What, then, shall we do with the other three and one-half years "left over?" We need not do anything at all. The point is that *within* the 70 heptads, or 490 years, the great work of salvation for the many would be accomplished by Messiah. He did so in 486.5 years. Fine!

With the completion of Messiah's work, the temple would no longer be necessary. Indeed, even in Daniel's time its importance had diminished. The exiles of Israel, sternly chastened, were purged of their heinous sin of idolatry. As a dispersed people, many of whom never got home, they longed for a greater salvation. The establishment of synagogue worship created a pattern for church worship for the New Covenant people of God. And, though a "Second Temple" was built at Jerusalem, true believers had learned that God was not confined to His "House" in His relationship with His people. The books of Ezekiel, Daniel, and Esther, in particular, describe Jehovah's very active presence with and on behalf of His exiled people.

As for the temple, the ripping of the veil that shielded the holy of holies while Jesus hung on the cross signified that God was through with the old sacrificial system. The shedding of Christ's blood, the blood of the New Covenant, fulfilled and replaced the Old. God in Christ brought in everlasting righteousness, putting His seal upon the promissory visions and prophecies. Jesus Himself pronounced judgment upon the city and the temple, which would henceforth come to symbolize the rejection of their Messiah by a majority of its people.[7] That earthly temple, rendered out of service, had to be destroyed. God would use Rome, as He once used Babylon, but this time with finality. The entire metallic image had collapsed. The "time of the end" had come; the old had passed away, the new had taken its place. The epistle to the Hebrews and the book of Revelation explain it all. As for Rome, as was earlier true for Babylon, we read: "Then what is decreed will be poured out on the destroyer" (end of v. 27).

Jesus forewarned His disciples of the coming catastrophe at Jerusalem, in terms of this very prophecy of Daniel. "Flee to the mountains," warns

7 See Matt 23:32-39 (Luke 13:34-35) and Matt 24:1-2ff.

Jesus, "when you see the abomination that leads to the desolation of which the prophet Daniel spoke." (Matt. 24:15-16; cf. Mark 13:14, as well as Luke 21:20-22, which describes the same setting, but in terms more clearly related to the coming of the [Roman] army to besiege and desolate Jerusalem.)

It is strange how some can see a postponement of the "Seventieth Week," when all that is said in Daniel fits so precisely with what Jesus came to do, and did indeed do. If our understanding of the purpose and meaning of Daniel's prophecy is new to you, please realize that it is not some new and strange doctrine. Many of the writers of the early church and of the Reformation, especially, saw Daniel's words in this same light. It is the theory of a postponement of the Seventieth Week that is the new and radical departure from historic Christian teaching. We believe what we have presented is what comes out of the Bible itself, the Old and New Testaments, and that the "futuristic" approach is something *read into* the text of Scripture.

By way of summation and clarification of what may still seem rather complex, if not downright bewildering, we present a "timeline" in chart form. As mentioned above, the struggles suffered by the Jewish state during the Greek period fit within the longest segment of "weeks," though this fact is not mentioned in the vision of chapter nine.

490 Years—in 70 "Weeks"

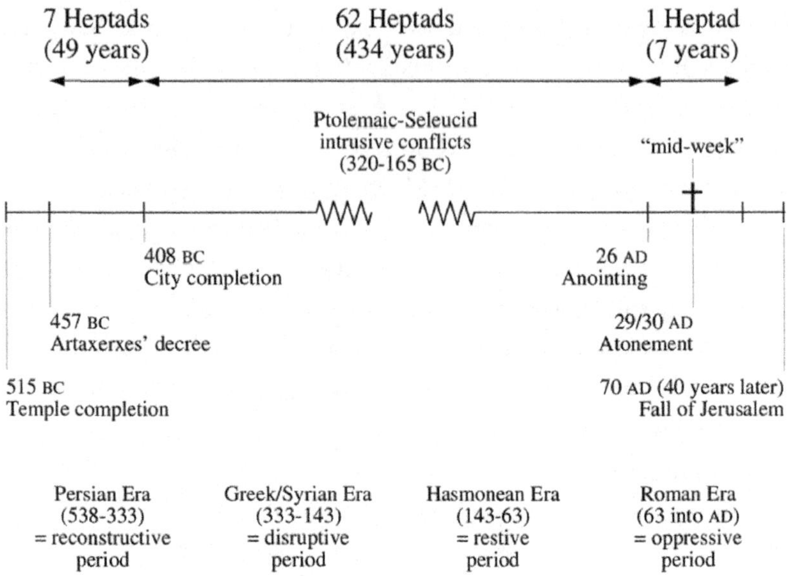

Chapters 10–11:19
Daniel's Final Vision

The then-aged Daniel received his final vision from God, and what a vision it is! How it came to him and what it was fills the last three chapters of his book. Actually, all this is but "one chapter," though it is traditionally divided into three. We've chosen to deal with it as one chapter in two parts. We want to highlight the climactic second part, while at the same time demonstrating the historical continuity of the whole picture.

Daniel tells us that he alone saw what appeared in the vision God gave to him. Those with him saw nothing (v. 7). Note that at the opening of the chapter, he had already called this extensive revelation a "word" or "matter," a *verbal* message that was "laid bare" to him in the third year of the reign of Cyrus. This message, in contrast to that forward look to the Messiah and to Jerusalem's fall at the close of chapter nine, deals with the interim period. It might well be called "The Wars of God and Men During the Greek Period," because it is set in the Hellenistic Age. All will become clear as we go on through these chapters.

Daniel was extremely moved by what he saw and heard on this occasion, just as we've seen him to be at other times when he was confronted with supernatural revelations. He tells us that he spent "three heptads of *days*" (in contrast to *years*, in ch. 9), meaning three weeks, "languishing, mourning" (literally sinking or drooping). Throughout those days he refrained from all fancy food and from the use of deodorant lotions.[1] The reason for the mention of a precise time period of twenty-one days will be seen shortly.

Notice that this time, as Daniel tells us in the first verse, he was given to understand the intent of this troubling message. It was a heavy

1 Necessary back then; they changed clothing infrequently!

matter. We see that "the word was truth, [about] a great warfare." What has pleased believers but proved to be a stumbling block and point of attack by skeptics is the amazing amount of detail with which events of the inter-testamental period are foretold. Apart from our belief that the 6th-century B.C. prophet Daniel wrote by divine inspiration, these precise predictions of what would occur in the fourth-to-second centuries prior to the birth of Christ, we would have to agree with the critics that someone wrote these chapters (or the whole book!) sometime around 165 B.C. They are too minutely accurate to known history to have sprung from human imagination. We'll deal later with the question of *why* all this needed to be revealed to Daniel after he received an answer to his basic question in chapter nine.

First, however, let's look at the astonishing circumstances under which the revelation was given to Daniel. So electric was the atmosphere associated with Daniel's vision that even though his companions could not see what he saw, "yet a great trembling befell them, and they fled into hiding" (v. 7).

What did Daniel see, then, as he stood by the bank of the River Hiddekel (Tigris)? His description sounds familiar to the New Testament reader:

> *When I looked up I saw, to my amazement, a man dressed in white linen, and his waist was belted in pure Uphaz gold. His body was like topaz of Tarshish, and his face like the appearance of lightning, his eyes like flaming torches, and his arms and lower limbs like the sparkle of polished bronze. The sound of his speech was like the sound of a large crowd.* (10:5-6)

Familiar? Yes. This vision is very similar to John's description of "One like the Son of Man" (his Lord Jesus), in Revelation 1:13-15. That title comes from Daniel 7:13, and the apostle must have also recalled these words of chapter ten. Was this, then, a preincarnation appearance of our Lord to Daniel, His beloved servant? It may well have been. The tone of the remarks of this impressive being, and the fact that he did not give his name as Gabriel (whom Daniel would have recognized) had freely done, would support that conclusion. Admittedly, it is possible that the Risen Christ purposely chose to come to His apostle by assuming an appearance resembling the mighty angel ("messenger") that was sent to Daniel some six centuries earlier. However, while we can't know for sure, it seems more likely that this was truly a *Christophany*, a preincarnation appearance on earth of the Second Person of the triune God.

Daniel's astounding visitor assured the prophet he had no need to fear, then went on to explain,

> *From the first day that you set your mind toward understanding and to humble yourself before your God, your words were heard, and I have come on account of them. But the prince of the kingdom of Persia stood against me twenty-one days. But take note, one of the chiefs of the princes, Michael, came to help me while I remained there, nearby the kings of Persia.*
>
> (vv. 12-13)

Now we see the significance of Daniel's reference to "three full weeks" in verses two and three. That was the duration of the forced delay in Persia of the messenger sent forth the moment Daniel had begun his quest. We are informed here of a warfare in the invisible, spiritual realm beyond our view.

There was a detaining, delaying, or thwarting of this messenger's approach to Daniel by a spiritual power favoring Persia. That may well be due to the fact that the true word or "decree" to be delivered involved the termination of the Persian Empire. "Don't *say* such a thing," was the mood of the resisters. In fact, this battle in the spirit realm had not yet ended. For in the last two verses of chapter ten we read this:

> *Then he said, Do you know why I have come to you? For now I shall return to fight with the prince of Persia; and just as I go out, the prince of Greece will enter.*
>
> *But I will tell you what is inscribed in the trustworthy record ("Book of Truth"); for there was not one who stood fast with me against these, except Michael your prince.* (vv. 20-21)

We learn here that this powerful person, who has come to Daniel first to strengthen him and then to place upon him a complex and burdensome message, was still on assignment. His words indicate that a struggle goes on in the spiritual world that determines the course of history on earth. Michael, the "archangel," had a special relationship to Old Testament Israel. We see that he took part in a supernatural battle which resulted in Greek victories over the Persians before the end of the fifth century BC, as well as in the full conquest of Persia by Alexander in 333 BC. Little Judaea could only sit by and watch.

How seriously Judaea would be affected by some international struggles in the period following Alexander is what the ensuing revelation to Daniel is all about. The obvious purpose for this, appended as it is to the longer range prediction of chapter nine, is to give divine reassurance to the Jewish nation. When they were to experience the havoc caused by foreign armies marching at will up and down their land, involving terrible persecution of the people and their sacred religion, they needed to know that it did not mean God's plans for them have gone awry. He has not forgotten them. They needed the assurance of God's own word (the Book of Truth) that things were right on track—for this set of events is just as He said it would be.

Before we move into the detailed prediction of what was yet to come, as given in chapter eleven, we must turn our attention once again to our poor old friend, Daniel. He'd been through a great deal over the years of his remarkable career. Next he was confronted, in response to his fasting and prayer, by a striking personage—a messenger sent from God, perhaps the Almighty Himself, as we explained above. Can we blame him for casting his glance to the ground and becoming speechless? Is it surprising that he complained of a total loss of strength, that he expressed confusion? Of course not. How else was a finite creature of dust to react when he met his God? We too should "take off our shoes," as it were, even in the reading of His Holy Word of authority and power.

Daniel was told in the middle of chapter 10 by the gleaming form dressed in linen what the subject of this vision would be. The one with a face "as the appearance of lightning" said, "I have come to inform you what will happen to your people in the latter days, for the vision concerns days yet to come" (v. 14).

The story begins by reviewing the start of Persian rule (following Cyrus will be Cambyses, Pseudo-Smerdes, and Darius I), with anticipation of what follows—down to the establishment and speedy division of Alexander's extensive empire. We read:

> *... Note that there are yet three kings determined for Persia; then a fourth will be rich, much richer than all of them, and by reason of the strength provided through his wealth he will stir all against the Greek realm.*
>
> *But a mighty king will stand up, and he shall rule with great dominion and act in accord with his own will. But even as he stands, his kingdom will be broken, divided to the four winds of the heavens—not for his posterity, nor in accord with dominion with which he had ruled—for his kingdom will be uprooted and belong to others besides those.* (11:2-4)

The rich king mentioned here was Xerxes, to whom Esther was married. Then once again we're brought to Alexander's conquests (that rough goat of ch. 8) and the splintering of his empire among four of his subordinates. Two of these were Seleucus, who claimed Syria (ancient Aram) and Mesopotamia, and Ptolemy, who retained his own satrapy of Egypt and North Africa. From the very earliest of their dynasties, the Egyptians considered the territory of Canaan Israel to be a "backyard" annex of Egypt. This made these two rulers next-door neighbors, but far from good neighbors.

At least a dozen times over the course of the next century and a half, the contending armies of the North (Syria) and the South (Egypt) marched detrimentally back and forth through the Holy Land. This was ever the convenient land bridge between the major powers of the ancient world. For His own purposes, God had placed His people where the action was. This is what we are witnessing as we read the end of Daniel's book.

The verses that follow verse 5 are truly amazing. So clearly identifiable from recorded history are the predictions made to Daniel, we can proceed by recounting those historical events, then simply make reference to the appropriate verses in Daniel. The reader will be amazed, and then come to realize how and why God told His servant Daniel all about what was to happen to his people three and a half centuries after his time.

In Egypt, Ptolemy I, named Soter, ruled for 38 years, beginning with Alexander's death in 323 B.C. His rule, however, proved to be weaker than that of another of Alexander's generals, Seleucus Nicator (meaning "Conqueror"), who first served Ptolemy but then established a stronger rival kingdom in Syria (v. 5). Allowing a gap of over 50 years, the prediction next centers on two new leaders. These are Antiochus II (Theos, "Divine") of Syria and Ptolemy Philadelphus of Egypt. The latter pressed Antiochus to divorce his wife Laodice and accept Berenice, the Egyptian's daughter, to seal an alliance between them. Two years later, when Ptolemy died, Antiochus put aside Berenice and took back Laodice, whose unassuaged resentment brought death to both her husband and her female rival, along with the whole Egyptian entourage which had accompanied Berenice to the north (v. 6).

Berenice's brother Ptolemy III (Euergetes) in turn conducted a successful invasion of Syria, establishing the temporary ascendancy of Egypt (v. 7). The carrying off of Syrian idols and wealth declares the victor's supremacy, allowing for a brief lull in the competition (v. 8). We must keep in mind that, with each of these encounters between the South and the North, troops were marching up and down the Palestinian land bridge, though the "Beautiful Land" is not mentioned in the biblical record until verse sixteen of our chapter.

The next Syrian ruler, Seleucus Callinicus (247–226 B.C.), conducted an unsuccessful expedition against Egypt (v. 9); but his sons, Seleucus III and Antiochus III (the Great) mounted an even stronger attack on Egypt (v. 10). The previously hedonistically preoccupied Egyptian ruler, Ptolemy Philopater, suddenly reacted bitterly with a military force with which he temporarily resisted the Syrian onslaught (vv. 11-12), only to fall in the end (v. 13). Both sides employed elephants in their military forces, but Antiochus gained the edge with a strong cavalry.

At this time some of the Jews, observing the weakened condition of their centuries-long irritant, those arrogantly intrusive Egyptians, got involved in the action under the leadership of a certain Tobias. This only served to invite the attention of their powerful pagan neighbors to the north. Thus their presumption proved to be foolish, but it was of God's design, and served to hasten the fulfillment of the visions given to Daniel about the sufferings to be endured by his people (v. 14).

The fortified city besieged by Antiochus (v. 15) was most likely Sidon, but his campaign extended southward to Gaza, which positioned him to control Jewish territory as well (v. 16). History also verifies that Antiochus III later sealed an alliance with Egypt by giving his daughter, Cleopatra I (the Cleopatra of Roman fame, paramour of Julius Caesar and Mark Anthony, was number VII), to Ptolemy V. Antiochus's expectations were thwarted; Cleopatra was loyal to her Egyptian husband, rather than serving her father's scheme (v. 17).

Antiochus the Great also turned his attention westward, seeking control of Asia Minor, the islands of Ionia, and even a part of Thrace. His boldness brought him into a direct clash with the aims of the Romans (vv. 18-19). A forceful reaction from Rome dealt him a decisive defeat at the hands of the Roman general Lucius Scipio.

Before we move on to the denouement of this remarkable preview of intertestament history given by verbal revelation to an astonished and befuddled Daniel, recall its purpose. All this was to reassure Daniel's future countrymen, those destined to live through a still more stressful series of events, that God knew well in advance exactly what was to transpire. He revealed even the thoughts and intents of those involved. His own people could rest assured that things were on track, not at all out of control.

Chapters 11:20–12
The Denouement: Mystery Unraveled

We have seen from history that events transpired in precise succession, exactly as God told Daniel they would. Now we must observe how all this was leading up to one major figure, the chief villain of the Greek period. Clear warning is given about the negative character and behavior of an especially aggressive and overbearing Syrian ruler. The unique nature of this particular king of the North was earlier pictured by the "little horn" that grew to be great, on the head of the male goat of chapter eight. (That horn, remember, is to be distinguished from the little horn of the fourth beast—Rome—in ch. 7. He was yet to be a featured evil one in the Revelation given the Apostle John.) The fog is lifting for us, even if it was not for poor Daniel.

As the story continues in chapter eleven of Daniel, verse 20 provides a transition. Yet what we find still concerned the running contest between the North and South. It prepares us for the entrance of the Syrian ruler who had the greatest impact upon the land and lives of God's people. Seleucus IV Philopator, who ruled 187-175 BC, had so much annual tribute demanded of him by Rome that he had to appoint a tough tax collector, Heliodorus, to extract wealth from nations that in turn were tributary to Syria. This included the rich treasuries of the Temple in Jerusalem. The reign of Seleucus IV, son of Antiochus the Great, ended with his death in a conspiracy that is said to have been engineered by Heliodorus. The throne did not pass down from Seleucus to his young son (a small child whose older brother was held hostage in Rome at the time), but to the late king's brother, Antiochus IV—the notorious "Antiochus Epiphanes," who ruled 175-164 BC. This ruler, the eighth

Seleucid ruler, whom we might call the "Antichrist" of the Old Testament, was the desecrator of the Temple of Jehovah God.

Here's how he was described to our perplexed friend, Daniel:

> *And a contemptible person shall stand in his place, though royal majesty had not been granted him, one who enters unexpectedly and seizes kingship by flatteries.*
>
> (11:21)

From the world's point of view, Antiochus IV was among the most elite of his day. He was enjoying the highly cultured atmosphere of Athens, Greece, up to the moment he slipped stealthily into his brother's royal shoes. The epithet "Epiphanes" he wore so proudly means "brilliant, glorious light." But so extreme was his egotistical showmanship (as was with Rome's Emperor Nero later on), extending even to the ascription of coins to Zeus pictured by his own likeness, many of his own subjects privately called him Antiochus Epimanes (meaning the "madman"). He was determined to completely Hellenize (Grecianize) the Holy Land, which was an aim diametrically opposed to the faith and practice of God's people.

From the day Antiochus assumed rule, a new and serious course was set. He continued the usual clashes with Egypt, but these now became incidental to the essential historical drama being viewed prophetically in the book of Daniel.

The next few verses (vv. 22-24) show us an ambitious ruler, who established political strength both by military might and international negotiations. Yet he acted so deceitfully that he gained few genuine supporters. We have a close modern parallel of bitter memory: the conniving dictator, Adolph Hitler.

At the heart of this brief passage is a rather incidental reference to a "prince of the covenant," who would also be "broken" as a consequence of the disruptions caused by this ambitious Syrian. In the context of Daniel's message to the faithful among the Jews, the office of high priest best fits to the title "prince of the covenant." At that time (175 BC), Jason, a pro-Syrian (Hellenized) brother of the more godly high priest Onias

III, secured his brother's office by sending bribes to Antiochus. Shortly thereafter, in 172, one Menelaus, who was not even of the Aaronic priestly line, offered a higher sum to gain the position and, for good measure, had Onias murdered.

Verses 25 through 27, which follow, describe the combat and dishonest negotiating between Syria and Egypt. Then verse 28 speaks of Antiochus' negative attitude and increasing hostility toward the holy covenant. He expressed his antagonism at this time by the sacrilegious plundering of the Jerusalem Temple. The reminder at the close of verse 27 (repeated in vv. 29 and 35), that the end would come at an appointed time, gives added assurance that God is still in control. These things would not continue unabated forever.

Trouble intensified when Antiochus mounted still another attack on Egypt. This time, another and even greater power entered the picture. Ships of Kittim (that is, from the direction of Cyprus) are a reference to the Roman party that confronted the Syrian as he besieged the Egyptian port of Alexandria. The Roman representative Popillius Laenas made Antiochus understand that the Senate of Rome stood opposed to a Syrian presence in Egypt. When Antiochus began to stall for time, the Roman legate scratched a circle in the sand around him. He demanded that Antiochus declare his intent before stepping out of the ring. Intimidated, the now humiliated king from the North relented rather than risking war with a far superior power (vv. 29-30).

Embittered by such insult and shame, Antiochus turned against the Jews in frustration on his way homeward. He resented those who had deep religious convictions and commitments so much at odds with his own worldly tastes and ambitions. On the other hand, he sought out those in Judaea who were forsakers of the covenant; those who were disloyal to Jehovah were therefore potential allies who would, for a price, support his wicked plans (v. 30).[1]

1 This much we learn from the prediction given to Daniel. A historical narrative provided in the fifth chapter of 2 Maccabees adds that while Antiochus was occupied in Egypt a false rumor of his death reached Jerusalem. This led to a rebellious conflict between parties there. As 2 Maccabees 5:11 tells it, "He therefore marched from Egypt, raging like a wild beast," and he stormed the city. 40,000 Jewish men, women, and children were reportedly slaughtered and an equal number sold into slavery.

The next few verses (31-35) carry us into the heart of what is an essentially spiritual warfare. With his own military forces and the cooperation of some apostate Jews, Antiochus did his worst against the House of God. The "wise ones," those righteous and valiant for truth, resisted, though many fell by the sword. The blood of martyrs then, as during early centuries of the church, throughout the Medieval and Reformation period, and on into our own generation, would be a sad but glorious attestation of loyalty to the Way, the Truth, and the Life. Daniel chapter twelve speaks of their everlasting reward.

The Temple itself was desecrated by Antiochus, who personally removed its golden vessels and robbed it of 1,800 talents, a tremendous amount of wealth. To put it mildly, he then added insult to injury when, in direct defiance of God, he sacrificed a pig on the altar and sprinkled its broth throughout the temple. Before returning to Syria, Antiochus made Jerusalem into a fortress for his troops. He was then determined to utterly stamp out the Hebrew religion. He forbade circumcision, burned all the copies of the Law of Moses he could find, and banned the offering of sacrifices to Jehovah. His most extreme act of sacrilege was to erect an idol of Jupiter in the Holy of Holies—"the abomination that causes desolation," or "the loathsome horror."

Among the faithful ones slaughtered were Mattathias and some of his sons, and the family that led the resistance, a God-fearing band known to us as the Maccabees. Though the Temple itself was cleansed and rededicated in three and a half years, it took 24 years of guerrilla warfare for the Jewish people to regain their independence in the year 143 BC. Pity this sorely oppressed nation as we may, we must also see that God was using a proud and blasphemous man from a pagan nation and culture to punish Israel for her sin and to purify a faithful remnant for His honor and use.

Verses 36 and following paint such a lurid picture of this man who represents Antiochus, that many commentators have jumped in their thinking to a time future to their own and to a personage belonging in the New Testament era. There is no reason for this conclusion, and it only confuses things. Whether or not we possess historical information dealing with the exact details about Antiochus in the latter part of chapter eleven, what is said well describes what we do know of his character and behavior.

The closing verses of chapter eleven (44-45) bring us right back to Antiochus Epiphanes anyway. They speak of his sudden departure to the east, upon report of a threat to his control in that region, and of his death there. This, in turn, ties in with what we are told at the end of chapter twelve. Daniel's final chapter opens with a clear statement that "*at that time*," the time of horrible desecrations, death, and destruction in Jerusalem, Michael, "who stands on behalf of the citizens of your people," would stand firm. He's the same angelic champion who had assisted the Spokesman (the Christ?) of Daniel's last three chapters against Persian opposition centered in the heavenly realm (10:13). This same pair, announced at the end of chapter ten, was ready to confront the "prince of Greece." In the predictions of the Book of Truth (see 10:20-21), this must refer to our Syro-Grecian villain, Antiochus Epiphanes, or to his sponsor in the demonic realm.

An important question was left unanswered in chapter eleven. What of the suffering saints, those faithful to God's laws in spite of the persecutions? (Compare the plea of the martyrs under the altar, in Rev. 6:10.) Chapter twelve *is* the answer. Michael, their protecting angel, would *at that time* deliver them. Then, the second and third verses parenthetically speak of their future and eternal blessed reward for that true and faithful witness. Notice that here we have specific reference to the resurrection of and contrasting awards for the righteous and wicked *of that time*, not to a general resurrection of all from all time. Their witness to God's truth makes them, literally, "righteous-makers of the many," or "justifiers of many." May we follow them with a similar witness in this chaotic world of our day.

Take note also that the wise (KJV "understanding") ones mentioned in 12:3 are the same as those spoken of in 11:32-33. In both places they are commended for doing the same thing—giving understanding (of God's purposes in all this) to many, even though they could fall victim to the evil assassin for it.

There is one seemingly elusive statement in the twelfth chapter of Daniel which is often misunderstood and therefore misconstrued. However, it is clearly related to these wise and righteous witnesses to the truth. Found at the end of verse four, the promise that many will "move to and fro," with the result that "knowledge will be increased," must be taken in its context. Daniel had just been ordered to shut up the words, to seal up his scroll for a time. "To the time of the end," to be precise. The traditional translation of "run to and fro" suggests a physical exertion, and the NIV's "go here and there" implies some sort of travel. The NASB's "go back and forth" better allows for what is a frequent sense of this verb in the Old Testament, the idea of *inspection*, as in examining or scrutinizing the passages of a written document. It was *at this time* of horrible suffering and of spiritual confusion that Daniel's book was to be opened. The seal could then be broken to reveal God's predictions and promises regarding this "time of distress, such as never has occurred ..." (12:1). Then, by going back and forth *in the prophecy*, they could understand God's ways with them.

The continuity of subject and the time frame of the last three chapters of the book of Daniel is made strikingly apparent in verses five and six of chapter twelve:

> *Then I, Daniel, saw—there stood two others! One was on this bank of the river and one on that. One said to the Man clothed in linen Who was above the waters of the river, "How much time to the end of these wonders?"*

The Man in linen (capitalized in allusion to His apparent deity) was still with Daniel, from 10:5 and on. He was the One with authority to answer questions posed by other (angelic) messengers. The reply is a clear and precise one. These devastating events, involving the temporary shattering of the power ("hand") of the saints of God ("holy people") to resist, were for a mercifully determined and shortened period: "a set time, times, and a half." This, as confirmed by historical record, speaks of the three and one-half years from the desecration of the Temple in 167 BC, to its liberation and cleansing by Judas Maccabaeus in December, 164.

Daniel pleaded for further clarification (v. 8), but he was told it was not his concern. The words are closed, sealed "until the time of the end."

Then what was described earlier (see 11:32-35) would occur: the wise would understand what was going on; none of the wicked would (v. 10). God told Daniel (v. 13) that he would have his rest (in death), with assurance that he too would share in the lot of the righteous (vv. 2-3) in the resurrection at the very end of the days.

Along with these words of caution and comfort to Daniel, further specification as to the time of crisis to be experienced by the saints of the intertestament period is given in verses 11-12. This puzzling set of numbers has led some to explain them figuratively and others to plot them into their "End Time" fantasies of speculative and sensational predictions of our own future. Nevertheless, when we keep in mind this entire segment of Daniel's Prophecy, the final three chapters being one unit—with Antiochus Epiphanes featured from 11:20 to the end—we can say, "No problem."

The 1,290 days of verse 11 give a more precise count to the three and a half year range for the Temple's desecration. The blessing for those who would abide another 45 days of stressful anticipation (the 1,335 days of verse 12) comes, doubtless, with the arrival of good news—a massive sigh of relief upon word of the death of Antiochus. The story of his renewed determination to turn Jerusalem into a mass grave for the Jews, thwarted by the fatal illness which overtook him as he sped westward by chariot upon word of the defeat of his troops by Judas Maccabaeus, is told in 2 Maccabees, chapters 8 and 9.

Thus we come to the close of Daniel's remarkable book. The lessons are clear-cut and positive: God is in control of the events of history, which itself moves in accord with His purposes and, in particular, in relationship to His people. Central to everything is the coming to earth of Jesus the Christ, God the Son, and the establishment of His kingdom—the only one which is forever, without end.

You can rest assured that in your personal life, in the affairs of our nation, and among the nations of the world, nothing is going to happen that has slipped out of or beyond God's control. If you have personal faith in the Redeemer, Christ Jesus, the Captain of our salvation, you too can go your way to the end of your days like faithful Daniel. You, along with him, can have confident assurance of resurrection victory, along with all those who have become wise through His Word.

John Calvin, writing during an unsafe period of the church's history, penned the following prayer at the end of his extensive commentary on the book of the Prophet Daniel:

> Grant, Almighty God, since thou proposest to us no other end than that of constant warfare during our whole life, and subjectest us to many cares until we arrive at the goal of this temporary racecourse: Grant, I pray thee, that we may never grow fatigued. May we ever be armed and equipped for battle, and whatever the trials by which thou dost prove us, may we never be found deficient. May we always aspire towards heaven with upright souls, and strive with all our endeavors to attain that blessed rest which is laid up for us in heaven, in Jesus Christ our Lord. Amen.

Praise be to God.

Appendix
The Words of Jesus in Matthew's Gospel

A Bridge Between Daniel and Revelation

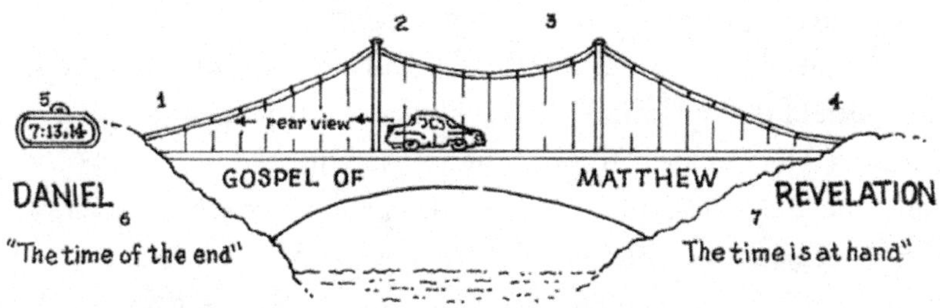

#1 Matthew 26:64

We drive onto the bridge at this verse, and a glance into the rear-view mirror tells us the source of what our Lord declares to the high priest at this highly dramatic moment of His trial. It comes directly out of Daniel's prophecy. Jesus Himself indicates the time of fulfillment for Daniel's words when He says, *'ap' 'arti*: "from just now, from now onward, henceforth." This shows the coming of the Son of Man on the clouds of heaven to sit at the right hand of the Power *in heaven* to be a part of the next major event in redemptive history. The sacrificial death, the bodily resurrection, *and* the ascension of Christ were about to transpire in rapid succession—in direct consequence of the reaction of Caiaphas to what He said. (Read vv. 57-66 to get the full picture.)

#2 Matthew 24:34

Another time sign is posted for us as we head for the center of the bridge. "This generation surely will not pass away until all these things take place," the Lord Jesus assures His anxious disciples. Read verses 23-35 to survey the scene. Notice in particular how "all these things" *includes* seeing "the Son of Man coming on the clouds of heaven with power and much glory." The teaching of Matthew 24, seen in its immediate context (the disciples' questions about the catastrophic demolition of Herod's magnificent temple structure), relates this manifestation and action of the reigning Son of Man to the judgment of the Jewish nation at the 70 AD destruction of Jerusalem (cf. Luke 21:20-28, where this very event is predicted in unmistakable detail).

The great significance of the Romans' destruction of Jerusalem and the Temple is largely overlooked. God had already spoken, in the splitting open of the veil of the Holy of Holies at the moment Jesus died on the cross. His prophets, from Moses to Malachi, had warned about the consequences of disloyalty to Israel's covenant God. Jesus Himself, with sorrow of heart, declared the end for Jerusalem. (See Matt. 23:37-38; Luke 13:34-35, and 19:41-44.) Jesus Christ, the Suffering Servant, died under brutal and ignominious treatment at the hands of both Jews and Gentiles; but as King of kings and Lord of lords, He would appear at the determined end of the Jewish age. He would then execute "the days of vengeance, in which everything that is written will be fulfilled" (Luke 21:22).

Admittedly, both the vision of Daniel (ch. 7) and the Olivet Discourse of Matthew 24 are widely interpreted as relating to the Second Coming of our Lord at the end of the church age, in which we are now living. But each passage of the Bible must be understood in its own contextual setting and interpreted by the comparison of one passage of Scripture with other pertinent ones, as to what is intended and being taught. Needless to say, there are seemingly incontrovertible references to Christ's bodily Second Coming in other passages such as John 14:1-4; Acts 1:6-11; Romans 8:18-25; 1 Corinthians 15:20-28; Hebrews 9:23-28.

#3 Matthew 16:28

Many have played around with the word "generation" found in our above-mentioned time sign (24:34). They attempt to stretch it on down through the centuries or to skip over all intervening centuries to make it fit their system of prophetic interpretation. But this parallel statement, at the end of Matthew 16, is unequivocal. "Let me assure you," says the Lord Jesus, "that there are some of those *who stand here* who will not taste death before they see the Son of Man coming in His empire."

It is true, as some are quick to point out, that three of the disciples got a foretaste of His glory at the mount of transfiguration (ch. 17, immediately following). But the verse must be seen in the context of what precedes it: "The Son of Man is going to come with His Father's glory along with His angels, and then He will reward each person according to his actions" (16:27). These words closely parallel what we saw in Matthew 24 as referring to the "rewards" (payment for unbelief and rebellion) meted out in the destruction of Jerusalem. Moreover, surely Jesus would not have made a point of some living long enough to see that day, were He referring to an event about to occur "after six days" (17:1).

#4 Matthew 28:18-20

Too often in the stressing of the Great Commission, verse 18 is overlooked. Yet it is essential to an understanding of the verses that follow. In fact, verse 18 sets forth the basis for the commission. It is *because* the Father gave His Son "all authority in heaven and on earth" that it was legitimate for Him to send the disciples forth as His messengers (*angels*) to all nations of the world to proclaim the good news.

Observe that the risen Lord announced to His disciples that "All authority ... *has been* given to Me"—completed action with present effectiveness. The "dominion" granted to Adam in the garden had been surrendered by him into the hands of Satan, who became "the ruler who has the authority of the air" (Ephesians 2:2) and "the god of this age" (2 Cor. 4:4; see also, John 12:31; 14:30; 1 John 5:19). This usurped authority was wrested from him by Jesus through His death and resurrection.[1] Then, He was about to ascend to the Father in clouds where, as the Son of Man, He would officially be given that dominion, glory, and a kingdom (Daniel 7:14) to which He already had claim. It would be "an everlasting dominion … which will not be destroyed" (Daniel 7:14).

#5 Daniel 7:13-14

This passage has been treated in the above paragraph, as well as in both the second and seventh chapters in the body of our book. But do keep one thing in mind. Nothing is more pivotal for understanding Daniel itself *and* for organizing the complex details of eschatology found throughout the Scriptures than your awareness that these two verses describe the return to glory of the Son of God incarnate. This was the answer to His prayer in the upper room, which included, "so now, Father, glorify Me with Yourself by the glory that I had before the world existed" (John 17:5).

#6 & 7 Daniel 12:4, 8, & 9; Revelation 22:10

Items six and seven of the diagram belong in proximity to one another. Together, they reinforce the foundations of our Matthew Bridge. Both passages speak of *time*, both speak of *books*, and both speak of *sealing*; both speak of these things in the last chapter of the prophecy. There can be little doubt, therefore, that John was thinking of Daniel 12 as he penned Revelation 22:10.

If you compare the passages from these two apocalyptic books, one major difference leaps from the pages. In Daniel, the command is to seal the words and the scroll "until the time of the end" (vv. 4, 9). In Revelation, the command given to John is: "Don't seal the words of the prophecy of this scroll" (Rev. 22:10).

---

1 The world of unregenerate sinners, of course, continues to serve the evil one, refusing to acknowledge Christ's kingship.

See the difference? Daniel was told that the prophecy (concerning Greece and Rome) pertained to the distant future. That's why he would not be able to understand it. So it was to be sealed up, awaiting *the* "time of the end," the time of those future world-kingdoms, the lower segments of the great metallic image. But John was told not to seal up the words of his book, because "the time is at hand." That is to say, the prophecy pertained to the immediate future. Jesus said, "See, I am coming soon, and My reward is with Me to pay each one according to his deeds" (22:12). That soon coming was fulfilled in 70 AD, Jerusalem's end, and in the decline and fall of the Roman Empire.